WILL THEY STAND

Parenting Kids to Face the GIANTS

KEN HAM

First printing: November 2020
Fourth printing: March 2022

Master Books®, P.O. Box 726, Green Forest, AR 72638
Master Books® is a division of the New Leaf Publishing Group, Inc.

ISBN: 978-1-68344-256-1
ISBN: 978-1-61458-766-8 (digital)
Library of Congress Number: 2020946139

Cover by Diana Bogardus

Unless otherwise noted, Scripture quotations are from the ESV® Bible (The Holy Bible, English Standard Version®), copyright © 2001 by Crossway, a publishing ministry of Good News Publishers. Used by permission. All rights reserved.

Scripture noted NIV is from the Holy Bible, New International Version®, copyright © 1973, 1978, 1984, 2011 by Biblica, Inc.™ Used by permission of Zondervan. All rights reserved worldwide.

Scripture noted NKJV is from the New King James Version, copyright © 1982 by Thomas Nelson, Inc. Used by permission. All rights reserved.

Scripture noted NASB is from the New American Standard Bible®, copyright © 1960, 1962, 1963, 1968, 1971, 1972, 1973, 1975, 1977, 1995 by The Lockman Foundation. Used by permission.

Please consider requesting that a copy of this volume be purchased by your local library system.

Printed in the United States of America

Please visit our website for other great titles: www.masterbooks.com.
For information regarding author interviews,
please contact the publicity department at (870) 438-5288.

Master
Books®
A Division of New Leaf Publishing Group
www.masterbooks.com

Dedicated to our family:

Our son Nathan and his wife Kristy, and their children Malachi and his wife Abigail, Kathryn, Noah, Madelyn, Emma, and Olivia. Our daughter Renee and her husband Bodie, and their children Kylie, Caleb, Lacey, and Lexi. Our daughter Danielle and her husband Joe, and their children Nicole, Kendra, Declan, and Lillianne. Our son Jeremy and his wife Susan, and their children Josiah, Amelia, Tiberius, and River Primrose (our #18 grandchild), and our "California girl," our daughter Kristel.

Ken and Mally Ham

Contents

PREFACE

Avery Foley,
writer and speaker with Answers in Genesis

- 94% of Belgian Doctors Support "After-birth Abortions" for Babies Born with Disabilities
- Pennsylvania District Mandates White Supremacy Lessons for Kindergartners
- California Legislators Approve Taxpayer-Funded Sterilization of Transgender Children
- Drag Queen Story Hour UK Reveals True Colors with "Love Has No Age" Tweet

By the time you read this, those headlines will be forgotten, replaced by even more startling, more extreme headlines as our Western culture dives deeper into the abyss of depravity. Freed from the once Christianized heritage that kept it moored to God's Word and a form of Christian morality, it seems with each passing day, our culture becomes more akin to the world before the Flood when "every intention of the thoughts of [mankind's] heart was only evil continually" (Genesis 6:5).

This is the world our children and grandchildren are growing up in. A world where drag queen story hours are just something that happens. Where taxpayers foot the bill for the mutilation of perfectly healthy organs as men yearn to "be" women, and women men. Where children with disabilities are discarded before, or after, birth. Where fighting racism means teaching it in a different form.

The title of Ken Ham's original book was *Raising Godly Children in an Ungodly World*. In our Western culture, we no longer live in "merely" an ungodly world — we are living in an anti-God world. Biblical teachings are mocked and reviled, slapped with the label of "hate speech." Those who believe the Bible, and live and act according to these beliefs, are vilified and face harassment, public censure, and slander for their stance. It's a hostile world, and Western nations are no longer the refuge they once were for those who believe the Bible.

How do we raise young men and women who will stand for biblical truth and the gospel in a world that just wants to silence them? In this book, Ken challenges parents (and this applies to grandparents as well!) to apply biblical principles to their most important job of all — discipling the next generation for Christ.

I had the sincere privilege of interviewing Ken's wife, Mally Ham, for chapter 11 of this book, as well as giving my thoughts on the initial manuscript and writing this preface at Ken's request. As a parent to three young children, I believe this book is a powerful resource and a loud wake-up call to parents to prayerfully consider the legacy they are crafting and to get back to the authority of God's Word and what matters most when it comes to parenting so we can raise a generation that knows what they believe, why they believe it, and can boldly stand on the gospel of Jesus Christ and the authority of the Word in a world filled with so many towering giants.

INTRODUCTION

Ken Ham

This is a very different book — certainly different from anything I've written so far. It is part journal, part tribute, part devotional, and part "how-to." It's also all heart, an expression of a passion, conviction, and commitment to the Word of God, all of which was instilled in me by my parents. It's very personal too, as I offer glimpses into my childhood, adult life, and a number of my life experiences. You will find these glimpses sometimes humorous, frustrating, or convicting, but as learning experiences for us all.

As I share with you journeys in the Ham family, you will see us, warts and all. I will share stories of being raised in Australia, a country that by anyone's standards would be considered non-Christian and pagan. I'll talk about my years as a student and a teacher, and about the surprising paths that brought me to where I am today as one of the leaders of the worldwide Answers in Genesis ministry. I'll even give you my bird's-eye view of the church as I've ministered in hundreds of churches worldwide — now that opens the door for some very interesting stories! Although I include many biographical details, this book is not a biography, but takes selected events from my upbringing to specially deal with the topic of raising godly offspring. I pray that the words ahead will bring glory to God for all He has done — and all He continues to do — for my family and yours as well.

In my capacity as a speaker for Answers in Genesis, I write and speak most often on topics related to the creation/evolution debate and Genesis. Over the years I have also developed messages about how the Genesis foundation (and the doctrines that are built upon it) impacts day-to-day life. I have come to understand that the battle over Genesis (particularly the history in Genesis 1–11) is not just about origins, it's about the foundation for our Christian worldview that affects every area of life.

I am greatly concerned with the condition of many church families. The statistics are discouraging, and the situation appears to be going from bad to worse, with the possibility that much of the coming generations could be entirely lost to the ways of the Lord. In the USA (and this is also true to an even worse extent in the rest of the Western world), only 11% of millennials (Generation Y) attend church weekly,[1] and it seems only 9%[2] of Generation Z are regular church attenders! And they are twice as likely to be atheist as any previous generation![3] As a result, the worldview of the culture is changing catastrophically. Because of my unique upbringing and understanding of the authority of the Word of God, I have been convicted to write this book in the hope that many more godly offspring will be produced for the Lord. I earnestly believe the trends we see can be reversed, one family at a time. But this is going to take some dramatic changes in many families.

To that end, this book is about the family — the Christian family. Specifically, I will do my best to answer this question: What does God's Word teach us regarding roles of parents and how to bring up children? As we find answers to these overriding questions, other important questions will be answered as well:

- Why is the family disintegrating?

1. "GSS Data Explorer: How Often Respondents Attends Religious Services," General Social Survey, accessed May 5, 2020, https://gssdataexplorer.norc.org/trends/Religion%20&%20 Spirituality?measure=attend.

2. George Barna, *Gen Z* (Barna Group and Impact 360 Institute, 2018), 26.

3. Ibid., 14.

- What is a godly legacy and why is it vital to our families and our society?

- What is God's purpose and meaning for the family?

- What is the primary importance of marriage?

- What are God's roles for the husband and wife in a family?

- How are we to train our kids and place ourselves in a position to answer our children's potentially faith-shattering questions?

- Is Christian education an option?

- Should all children be homeschooled?

- Are Christian children meant to be salt and light in the public schools?

- What is the state of Christian education?

- How are we to implement godly discipline and teach our children discernment?

- What is happening to the modern church?

The answers to these vital parenting questions (and many, many more) are found in the Bible, starting with the Book of Genesis. The sufficiency and authority of Scripture, properly interpreted and understood, gives us the basis for godly parenting.

As you take God's Word and apply its eternal principles to the everyday issues you face with your family, you will begin to create a godly heritage — a legacy that will impact the generations to come in ways you never dreamed possible.

I am, by God's grace, the head of a major Christian organization, and an author of many books. Through our websites, conferences, radio programs, and written literature, and our two major themed attractions, the Creation Museum and the Ark Encounter, God is using the ministry of Answers in Genesis to influence tens of thousands of lives throughout the world on a daily basis. As I address these vital topics regarding parenting, I will share, as best I understand them, the influences which have guided my life and shaped me into who I am today. I will also lay down the biblical foundation for raising godly children that I have learned from my parents and with my godly wife over many years. As I share all this with you, it is my hope that these personal words will challenge us concerning the legacy we are leaving in our children. I pray you will be equipped to train up a generation that will stand on God's Word with boldness and will not be intimidated by the secularist giants that come against them.

CHAPTER ONE

LEAVING A LASTING LEGACY

A good man leaves an inheritance to his children's children (Proverbs 13:22).

∾

On the northern tip of Australia lies a nondescript outpost called "Thursday Island." Sparsely inhabited by indigenous people from Papua New Guinea, and surrounded by the deep blues of the sea, the small and quiet community serves as the commercial center for the Torres Strait Islands, a small cluster of tropical islands just off Cape York.

On the 22nd of October, 1928, a child came into the world on this little-known island, his birth going unnoticed by all except a few. It was an unremarkable entrance into human existence, in an unremarkable location, far from the cities and headlines that concerned the rest of the world at that time.

The second of two children, the child grew through humble means and hard work in a land that was raw and full of potential. As the son of an educator, he learned his lessons well, many of them the hard way. He made music upon the violin and banjo mandolin and learned his three R's by the light of a gas lamp when the day was through.

When he was 16, his father died. With no earthly father to guide him into adulthood, he turned to his Heavenly Father for direction, stability, and a model after which to shape his life. In the words of the Bible he found all he needed; the Book fed both his passion for learning and his heart for his Lord and Creator. In the hospital just before his father passed into glory on the 9th of June, 1995, my late brother Robert asked him a question: "Dad, why did you love God's Word so much?" His answer: "After my earthly father died, I then turned to the words of my Heavenly Father and read them over and over again." Dad saturated himself in the Word of God.

As the world began to heal from the wounds of World War II, the son of the educator chose to become an educator himself, investing his career in the next generation as a teacher, administrator, and principal. With his new bride in one hand and his Bible in the other, he set out to make an eternal difference in his world. As his passion for truth and the lost continued to grow, he became a powerful and articulate defender of his faith and the Word he so desperately loved, in his home, his schools, his church, and his community.

Then, on October 20, 1951, in the northern town of Cairns, he did a most remarkable thing: He became a father — but not just any father; he became *my* father — the man I will forever call "Dad." On the day I was born he became the most important man I would ever know on the face of this earth.

With a family now in tow, and the decades beginning to slip away, he seized every day as an opportunity to influence his world for truth and to shape his children into those who would love God and His Word. Through his words and through his life, he imparted lessons that will be forever etched in my mind and in the hearts of my four living siblings, and in the heart of my late brother Robert (who was a great teacher of the Word): **Whatever you do, you do it 100 percent.**

Dad never did anything half-heartedly. If it was worth doing at all, he did it as best he could. His reports as an educator were first class; his interaction with students and other teachers was always focused and intentional. He had chosen to serve the world as an educator, but he approached the task with an intensity that reflected the truth in Colossians 3:23–24: "Whatever you do, work heartily, as for the Lord and not for men, knowing that from the Lord you will receive the inheritance as your reward. You are serving the Lord Christ."

In those days, Australian educators were transferred every few years as they climbed the promotional ladder. Approximately every three years or so we would pack up the family and move to a different location throughout the state of Queensland. Finally reaching the top as a principal of a class 1 school, we settled down in the city of Brisbane, where he continued his work and his parenting with passion and devotion.

What you do at the top filters down and brings others up. Dad showed us that a leader has responsibility, because those who follow are greatly influenced by the one out in front. In Luke 6:40, Jesus said: "A disciple is not above his teacher, but everyone when he is fully trained will be like his teacher."

By his example, Dad illustrated this truth in clear ways, both in his schools and in our home.

Who we are impacts those in our charge, either for good or for bad. While other principals (and many teachers) hit the pub after work and wondered why their teachers were sluggish in the mornings, Dad upheld his moral integrity . . . and his teachers and faculty followed. His schools were simply the best in the territory.

Invest where it counts. Through our parents, we learned about godly generosity. Our house was a well-known stopping-off point for missionaries, and Mum and Dad freely gave whatever assistance they could to ministers of the Word — they had such passion to see the gospel proclaimed and people saved. On one occasion, a missionary needed money to continue his journey, and my parents gave him the little they had, never letting on what a phenomenal sacrifice it was for them.

If my parents acquired some household goods, resulting in them not needing a piece of furniture or some other item, they would look for a needy person to give the excess piece. Generous with their finances, possessions, and time, they always exhibited such joy in helping others. They understood and practiced Matthew 6:19–21:

> Do not lay up for yourselves treasures on earth, where moth and rust destroy and where

> thieves break in and steal, but lay up for your-
> selves treasures in heaven, where neither moth
> nor rust destroys and where thieves do not
> break in and steal. For where your treasure is,
> there your heart will be also.

As their children, we recognized that the Lord is good and generous, so why not help others? Where did I learn that? Mum and Dad for sure.

Take action and take risk. Dad was a risk taker and a man of action. He and Mum never really wondered how to get something done, they just did it. Whether it was bringing missionaries into town for a campaign, starting a Sunday school, or giving more than they reasonably should, they rarely counted the costs. If they felt the burden that something should happen, they made it happen. They were like Nehemiah, who, when he saw the walls of Jerusalem and the temple of God in ruins, was burdened to do something about it. When he saw the leaders treating the people unjustly, he asked the question, "Why isn't someone doing something?" He acted and took it upon himself to rebuild the holy city and ensure justice for the people. Daniel 11:32 says: ". . . but the people who know their God shall stand firm and take action."

My father and mother were known as people of strength and action, even when the task before them was filled with great risk. Did this affect us as their children? Of course it did. When they took risks and acted, we saw time and time again the provision of God, giving us the faith to act as well. Like my father, I've been a risk taker, too. When I look at the history of Answers in Genesis, I just shake my head. I don't know how we did it back then, and I don't know how we are doing it now. The people involved, the growing vision, the incredible provision of God every time we take a step . . . it's miraculous, I think. I doubt I ever would have learned to take risks (which are really just steps of faith, carefully and prayerfully thought through) and to take action had I not grown up with the model of my parents.

Defend the faith wherever you might be. Australia is quite a large country, about the same size as the 48 states of the continental United States. The population, however, is rather small, currently about 25 million. It is a land of rich natural resources, but spiritually, it is a dry, dry desert. The number of true born-again Christians in my homeland is probably only 1 or 2 percent. Only a maximum of 16 percent attend churches of any kind regularly.[1] In this land of great spiritual need, our parents instilled in us the conviction to be missionaries and defenders of the faith, no matter where we happened to be.

Some of the small towns we were transferred to only had one or two churches, and sometimes there were no Sunday schools at all in the rural areas where Dad's school was located. I remember my parents starting up Sunday schools so they could reach children with the truth of God's Word and the gospel. Sunday after Sunday they would drive from house to house, picking up kids and packing them in the car like sardines . . . with no seatbelts, of course. (I know, you could get arrested for that today, but back then it's just what they did to do what they knew had to be done.)

The lack of churches in the cities we lived in often made it difficult to find one that stood on the authority of God's Word. Not all the churches we attended had pastors who took the stand they should have on God's Word. Many times, I recall my father, with my mother and us children in tow,

---

1. McCrindle, "Faith and Belief in Australia," accessed May 5, 2020, https://2xnd9o36f4oj3bqjpe25jqfz-wpengine.netdna-ssl.com/wp-content/uploads/2019/09/Faith-and-Giving-in-Australia-Report-digital.pdf.

going up to the pastor after a service. With Bible in hand he would calmly challenge the pastor about some of the things he said in his sermon, quoting Scriptures that resounded with the phrases "Thus said the Lord" or "It is written. . . ." Dad just loved the passages that proclaimed, "Thus says the Lord," "It is written," and "Have you not read. . . ?" (To this day, when I quote verses that contain these phrases, an image of my father confronting liberal pastors pops into my mind!)

As we were transferred around, my father served on many different deacon/elder boards of churches throughout the state of Queensland. I gained an interesting perspective on the church as we attended churches including Brethren, Presbyterian, Methodist, and Baptist. Often Dad would come home from a meeting really upset that someone didn't seem to want to take a stand on issues he believed were vital. Whether it was Sunday school material, mission outreach, or discipline that needed to be applied to a wayward member, my father wanted to do what God's Word clearly taught, but many times others in leadership didn't want to "rock the boat," or they wanted to smooth over the situations without confrontation. Not our dad. He wasn't afraid to shake things up when necessary. I heard them call Dad "Merv the stirrer" because he didn't hesitate to jump in and ruffle some feathers if the integrity of the Word was at stake.

Was he correct in all instances? Probably not, and I'm not even aware of all the situations he was involved in. Even if my father wasn't always right in every situation, I know his heart was in the right place every time. To the best of his understanding, he wanted to do things God's way. If that meant being called a "stirrer," then so be it. He put God's Word before losing church members or friends if someone needed confronting in a biblical manner.

We learned that vital lesson well as his children, and it's important that you do the same. If you take the Bible seriously, live by it, and defend it when it is compromised, you will likely be tarred with the same brush. I have experienced the same stereotyping as my father from certain people over the years from both secularists and those in the church. No matter how graciously you put across scriptural truth, you will also potentially be viewed in a similar manner.

Yes, Dad was considered a "boat rocker," and he was prepared to make waves when necessary. He felt that if you needed to create a tsunami to make things right, then so be it. Sure, he cared about what people thought of him, he cared about them very much . . . but he cared about the Bible more. The Word of God was the foundation of his life. It was the air in his lungs and the blood in his veins. He never ceased to read it, contemplate it, apply it, and defend it. In 2 Timothy 4:1–5, Paul exhorted Timothy with a great challenge, a challenge that my father accepted as his own:

> I charge you . . . preach the word; be ready in season and out of season; reprove, rebuke, and exhort, with complete patience and teaching. For the time is coming when people will not endure sound teaching, but having itching ears they . . . will turn away from listening to the truth and wander off into myths. As for you, always be sober-minded, endure suffering, do the work of an evangelist, fulfill your ministry.

Daily, he would study and study so he could be prepared to defend the Christian faith against false teaching and the claims that the Bible contained contradictions. Whether it was the worldwide Flood, the feeding of the 5,000, or arguing against the possibility that man evolved from molecules to an apelike creature to man over millions

of years, Dad defended the Word of God as if his
life depended upon it . . . which, in fact, it did.
Many years later, I realized he was an apologist,
teaching his family answers (apologetics) to defend
the Christian faith against the attacks of that time
that would undermine the authority of the Word of
God. I also came to understand that he was teaching me to think foundationally — that God's Word
is the foundation for our entire worldview.

He was always very adamant about one thing
— if you can't trust the Book of Genesis as literal
history, then you can't trust the rest of the Bible.
After all, every single doctrine of biblical theology is founded in the history of Genesis 1–11. My
father had not developed his thinking in this area
as much as we have today at Answers in Genesis,
but he clearly understood that if Adam wasn't created from dust, and that if he didn't fall into sin as
Genesis states, then the gospel message of the New
Testament can't be true either.

When it came to apparent contradictions or
scientific conflict, he would say something like this:
"Kenneth, even though I don't have the answers
in this area doesn't mean there aren't any — it just
means we don't have them at this time. We need to
ask God to provide us with answers — but even if

he doesn't, this is no reason to reject God's Word." Dad (and Mum) hated compromise, and such a stand has had a lasting impact on my life.

Dad, by example and through his teaching, had helped me understand something that has been with me since that time: When something we learn contradicts Scripture, we need to first of all go to the Bible and study the words in context very carefully. If, after doing this, we are sure the Bible still clearly means what we had previously gleaned, then we need to question the ideas that contradict the Bible's words. Then, even if we can't find an explanation that shows where the secular idea is in error, we need to continue to search and wait for the answer. Even if we don't find answers in our lifetime, we cannot reinterpret Scripture. To do so would be to make man's ideas infallible and God's Word fallible. This would put us on a course of compromise and unbelief through the rest of Scripture, and Dad often warned us of this "slippery slope." This lesson I learned I believe is a major reason why Answers in Genesis has stayed the course. Sadly, many Christian organizations and churches have drifted away from God's Word as they have reinterpreted Scripture to fit with the changing culture of our day. No! We must judge the culture based on the absolute authority of the Word of God. Thanks, Dad, for drumming this into me. My favorite photo of my Dad is of him with his Bible open in his lap teaching others:

These were some of the lessons learned from my parents — lessons that shaped my life in every way and continue to shape the lives of our children and those around us. God used them both to impact our lives as children, in ways we still cannot imagine. In the end, their example taught us vital priorities: We learned that life was to be lived with God first, others second, and self third.

Throughout my childhood and teenage years, two aspects of Dad's life made impressions on me more than all the others. First, he hated compromise. He would never knowingly compromise the

Word of God, and he took the scriptural warnings about compromise, purity of doctrine, and contending for the faith very seriously.[2] After all, he had saturated himself in the Word of God, so he knew what it taught. Second, he obeyed the pointed command made in 1 Peter 3:13–15:

> Now who is there to harm you if you are zealous for what is good? But even if you should suffer for righteousness' sake, you will be blessed. *Have no fear of them, nor be troubled*, but in your hearts honor Christ the Lord as holy, always being prepared to make a defense to anyone who asks you for a reason for the hope that is in you; yet do it with gentleness and respect [emphasis added].

Okay, in all honesty, he sometimes forgot about the "gentleness" part (none of us Hams will ever claim he was perfect!), but he had the rest of the passage down firm. He would stand up strongly for what he believed was true. He was a leader who listened to advice, but he was never intimidated by people who weren't willing to suffer in order to stay true to the Word of God. He was a man of

2.   See Ps. 18:30, 56:4, 103:20, 119:1–176; Matt. 12:5, 19:4, 22:31; Mark 12:10; Luke 6:3; Phil. 1:10; 1 Tim. 1:5; 1 Pet. 1:22.

great conviction with a deep passion for the Word of God.

He was an uncompromising witness and defender of the gospel. God used him to lay a rock-solid foundation for our family and prepare us not only for this present life — but also for an eternity with our Creator. I cannot fathom the value of this inheritance which he left me. There is no doubt in my mind that the legacy of my father and mother, together with the Lord's calling on my life, is the reason I came to be in the ministry of Answers in Genesis — now reaching millions of people around the world. And I have to add that the ministry would not be where it is today without the sacrificial dedication of my godly wife, Mally (and Nannan to 18). That's a book in itself.

Who would have guessed that God would use a simple man like my father to shape our family in such powerful ways? Who could have speculated that through the faithful obedience of a boy from Thursday Island and the humble devotion of my dear late mother, God would choose to make such an impact on the world?

They were simple vessels that served a mighty God. As their child and His, I will be eternally thankful to the One who loaned them to me, who guided them with His Word, and who empowered them with His Spirit to raise a godly family in an ungodly world.

> . . . he who is the blessed and only Sovereign, the King of kings and Lord of lords, who alone has immortality, who dwells in unapproachable light, whom no one has ever seen or can see. To him be honor and eternal dominion. Amen (1 Timothy 6:15–16).

#18 arrived

DEAD MEN

DO TELL TALES

For the righteous will never be moved;
he will be remembered forever (Psalm 112:6).

∾

There is a saying, one that we have gathered from the legends of the Wild West, which says "Dead men tell no tales." The saying implies that the knowledge and influence of the deceased goes with them to the grave, never to be heard from again. I find that not to be the case! Dead men do tell tales. If you ever take a walk around the small English town of Bedford, as I have, you will quickly see what I mean.

legacy (lĕg´e-sē) n. Something handed down, by one who has gone before in the past, and left to those in the present and future.

Bedford was the hometown of John Bunyan, author of the still very popular *Pilgrim's Progress*, now in its 400th year of printing.[1] The day I walked around the town, I saw reminders of John Bunyan everywhere — the site of the jail where he spent many years imprisoned, the site of the house in which he was raised, his statue in the town square, the church he preached at in later life with a museum of many of his personal items, and the church where he was baptized in 1628. Bedford even has a pub called "Pilgrim's Progress Pub"! (I'm sure John Bunyan would love to know he had a pub named after his famous book!)

Something really hit me as I walked around Bedford. As I thought about the life of John Bunyan and how he was persecuted and jailed for preaching the Word of God, I wondered about what happened to those responsible for his persecution and jailing. There was no mention of any of Bunyan's enemies in Bedford. In fact, in the large graveyard of the church where Bunyan rang the church bell as a child, I saw many very old gravestones. It is certainly possible that some of these gravestones stand on the graves of Bunyan's persecutors. However, these gravestones were so eroded that the names

---

1. *The Pilgrim's Progress* was published in 1678.

had disappeared. Whoever these people were, their memory has all but gone. As I looked at these nameless gravestones, Proverbs 10:7 came to mind: "The memory of the righteous is a blessing, but the name of the wicked will rot."

Certainly, this is the case in Bedford. The man who stood for the authority of the Word of God is remembered. The memory of those who opposed Bunyan has disappeared into oblivion. Bunyan and his books (particularly *The Pilgrim's Progress*) live on in the memories of people all over the world and in the printed pages that still come off the printing presses today. Yes, the righteous "will be remembered forever."

A very similar type of situation exists in the town of Worms, Germany. My wife, Mally, and I walked around this town, finding many memorials to Martin Luther, the great reformer who started the Reformation in 1517.[2] There were

2. On October 31, 1517, Martin Luther nailed the 95 Theses to the door of the Castle Church in Wittenberg, Germany.

various statues, plaques, and other markers that told the story of Martin Luther. I even had the awesome opportunity to stand at the very place where it is believed Luther stood when he was purported to have uttered these now famous words: *Here I stand [on scripture]. I can do no other. God help me! Amen.*

I must admit, tingles went down my spine as I stood there and contemplated the life of a man who started a movement that has affected the world for the Lord to this day.

Again, I didn't see any memorials to all of those who opposed Luther. They aren't remembered in Worms; the memory of those who persecuted him is all but lost. Luther — the man who stood for the authority of the Word of God — is remembered, and his legacy continues to have great impact on the world today . . . even among those who don't know his name. The righteous shall be in everlasting remembrance, but unfortunately, the unrighteous can still make an everlasting impact as they forge legacies of an entirely different kind.

If you walk the streets of Shrewsbury, England, you will find memorials to another man of great influence — memorials quite similar to those left for Bunyan and Luther. There is a statue outside his school and a sign outside of the home of his birth, noting the date of February 12, 1809. This is the birthdate of Charles Darwin, who at the age of 50 would publish *On the Origin of Species*. Through-

out the town a similar pride is felt and is reflected in the names of many locations: Darwin Gardens, Darwin Terrace, Darwin Street, and Darwin Shopping Centre.

There are similarities in the memorials to these three men, but the legacies they left behind could not be more different. Darwin proposed that all life can be explained by natural processes without God. By concluding that a supposed link between ape-like creatures and man meant that there is no God (as detailed in his subsequent book, *The Descent of Man*), his ideas left humanity to decide right or wrong on their own, to write their own rules and do their own thing, following whatever seems best in their own eyes. Really, Darwinian evolution is the pagan religion of this age attempting to explain the origin of life by natural processes. We need to understand that naturalism is, in essence, atheism.

The implications of Darwin's legacy are far-reaching. He paved the way for moral relativism, and he fueled racism (claiming that blacks, Aborigines, and others are inferior, less-evolved races.[3]) His ideas have also helped fuel the abortion industry, leading to the conclusion that an unborn child is nothing more than a clump of cells (or just an animal) and that a woman has the right to kill (actually murder) it if she so chooses. The ideas

3. Charles Darwin, *The Descent of Man* (London: John Murray, 1882), 156.

of Darwin even paved the way for Hitler, whose devotion to evolution convinced him it was the only real basis for national policy,[4] and he used these ideas to justify the extermination of those he considered less than ideal — resulting in the mass murder of millions of Jews, gypsies, and others. Here in the USA, one of the students involved in the Columbine (Colorado) school shootings of 1999 wore a T-shirt with "natural selection" written on it. And this makes sense — the more students are told they are just animals and have evolved by natural processes, the more they will begin to act consistently with this view of origins.

Darwin's ideas have contributed to the erosion of the family, educational institutions, the decay of the legal system, and have led to great compromise in the Church. As generations are trained to believe there is no God, thus no absolute authority, then there is no basis for determining right and wrong — moral relativism will pervade the culture. And we see this happening catastrophically throughout the once very Christianized Western world.

The late Dr. Carl Sagan and his wife, Ann Druyan, wrote an article that appeared in *Parade*

---

4.   Arthur Keith, *Evolution and Ethics* (New York: G.P. Putnam's Sons, 1947), 28.

Magazine on April 22, 1990, using the fraudulent idea of embryonic recapitulation popularized by Ernst Haeckel (the false idea that when an embryo develops in its mother's womb it goes through a fish stage, etc., reflecting its evolutionary history, until it becomes human) to justify abortion. They claimed the embryo wasn't really human until about the sixth month.

I've heard of girls who were told by an abortion clinic that what was in their womb was in the fish stage of development, thus they could abort it. A false view of origins leads to terrible consequences.

This is the Darwinian legacy: a false idea that has led to the destruction of the authority of the Word of God in our modern age. He popularized a philosophy that has convinced others that the Bible is not true; that everything is the result of random natural processes; and that we are little more than animals, free to decide as we are bidden to decide.

As this book is dealing with the topic of parents and the training of children, and as I mentioned Carl Sagan above, I believe it important to show a sad fruit of his (and his wife's) legacy. The daughter of this famous scientist, Carl Sagan, who was known for saying, "The cosmos is all that is or was or ever will be," wrote a book in 2019 where she details her search for meaning and purpose.

In an interview about the book,[5] we are reminded of the ultimate meaninglessness and purposelessness of the totally bankrupt religion of naturalistic evolution as Sasha Sagan attempts to create meaning for life in a worldview with no ultimate basis for it. It's also a reminder of how important it is for parents to teach their children the truth of God's Word and arm them with answers to the skeptical questions of the day that attack God's written Word.

In the interview, she says things such as "For me [the meaning of life is], the love I feel for my husband, for our daughter, for our family and friends. Feeling those moments of joy and appreciation for being alive. It's also the deep sense of fulfillment I get from learning as much as I can, from understanding, from connecting dots, learning how interwoven life on our planet really is." Her answer really borrows from the Christian worldview in

---

5. Alita Byrd, "Carl Sagan's Daughter on Science and Spirituality," *Spectrum Magazine*, November 12, 2019, accessed May 5, 2020, https://spectrummagazine.org/interviews/2019/carl-sa-gans-daughter-science-and-spirituality.

using words like "love," "joy," etc. The interview clearly shows that those who reject God have a type of faith, but it's a blind-faith religion, and for them, "purpose" and "meaning" only apply to the here and now while they're alive. After that comes "dreamless sleep," which means when you die, you're done, never to be conscious again! And this is the state religion presented in the public school system and secular media!

Carl Sagan's daughter was clearly trained in atheistic evolutionary cosmology by her parents! How we need godly parents to train up a generation of godly offspring! Fathers, bring your children up in the "discipline and instruction of the Lord" (Ephesians 6:4). Don't leave a legacy in your children as Sagan has.

Now, back to Darwin. Two signs outside of the Shrewsbury Unitarian Church in his hometown speak for themselves. The first proudly proclaims: *Charles Darwin worshiped here when he was young.* This church celebrates that a man who did so much to undermine the truth of God's Word once attended their church!

The second church sign gives a clear indication of the legacy behind which the legacy of Darwin

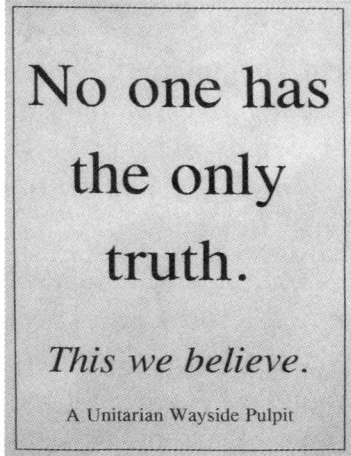

No one has
the only
truth.

This we believe.

A Unitarian Wayside Pulpit

emerged: *No one has the only truth, this we believe.* It's no wonder they celebrate Darwin's sad legacy— this "church" refuses to accept God's Word as the authority and instead embraces the secular idea that truth is relative.

Not a Question of "If"

Luther, Bunyan, and Darwin: these three men left two entirely different kinds of legacies. Each legacy continues to impact the world in different ways. Let there be no doubt: A legacy is a very, very powerful thing. Let there be no doubt about this either: You too will leave a legacy. Truly, it's not a question of if you will leave a legacy, it is only a matter of what kind. Long after your body is laid to rest, the impact of your life will continue to spread throughout your community and your world. Never forget that your legacy will be felt most strongly by those closest to you: your family.

Your family desperately needs you to stand up and lead because the world is drawing them in all the wrong directions. Statistics indicate that around 90 percent[6] of the children from church homes attend public schools in America. Sadly, statistics indicate that seven out of ten of such students will walk away from the church after their senior high years.[7] And one of the major reasons we discovered through our research was that they weren't really taught apologetics so they would

---

6.   Daniel J. Smithwick, "Teachers, Curriculum, Control: A 'World' of Difference in Public and Private Schools," (Lexington, KY: Nehemiah Institute, Inc., 1999), 11.

7.   T.C. Pinckney, "We Are Losing Our Children," Remarks to Southern Baptists Convention Executive Committee, September 18, 2001. Also, Barna Research Online, "Teenagers Embrace Religion but Are Not Excited About Christianity," January 10, 2000, www.barna.org/cgi-bin/PagePressRelease. asp?PressReleaseID=45&Reference=D – states: "When asked to estimate the likelihood that they will continue to participate in church life once they are living on their own, levels dip precipitously to only about one of every three teens."

know the answers to the skeptical questions that attacked the authority of God's Word beginning in Genesis.

America is said to have been the greatest Christianized nation on earth. This country has the world's greatest number of Christian bookshops, Christian radio stations, churches, seminaries, and Christian and Bible colleges. It is inundated with all of the best Christian resources available, yet America is becoming less Christian every day from a worldview perspective . . . and many Christian parents/grandparents are heartbroken to see their children and grandchildren move toward the world and away from the church.

Dads and moms are crying out for answers, and teachers are becoming increasingly concerned by the rebellious attitudes, lack of politeness, and vanishing Christian morals they see, even in "church kids." Barna Research found that only nine percent of teens who call themselves "born-again Christians" believe in absolute moral truth.[8] Family breakups, even among those calling themselves Christian, are

---

8. Barna Research Online, "The Year's Most Intriguing Findings, from Barna Research Studies," December 12, 2000, www.barna. org/cgibin/PagePressRelease.asp?PressReleaseID=77&Reference=E&Key=moral%20truth.

startlingly common.[9] What are the problems? What are the solutions? Are there answers that will deal with the heart of the problems and provide real solutions? Christian and secular books about the family and raising children abound, yet the questions continue. How should children be raised in today's world? How can a family produce godly offspring dedicated to the Lord? What methods of discipline should be used in bringing up children? Should Christian children be kept in public schools to witness to others, or is Christian school or home-school a necessity? How can Christianity be made relevant to the younger generations?

The list of questions goes on and on, and the Christian family of today is deeply struggling to find answers. I believe there are answers — but I want to warn you that they may challenge your comfort zone, and they may go against what is "acceptable" in your community and even your church. The answers may be labeled as "offensive" to those who are more worried about political correctness than righteousness.

---

9   Barna Research Online, "The Year's Most Intriguing Findings, from Barna Research Studies," December 12, 2000, www.barna. org/cgi-bin/PagePressRelease.asp?PressReleaseID=77&Reference=E&Key=divorce. "Born-again adults are more likely to experience a divorce than are non-born again adults (27% vs. 24%)."

Before you can even begin to search out and apply the answers, even more fundamental questions must be answered: What kind of legacy do you intend to leave? What type of memorials might be left in your remembrance?

Can I humbly suggest that you can leave a memorial that can affect the world as Luther and Bunyan did? Many of you reading this might be saying, "Give me a break! They were great and now very famous men. They deserve such memorials, but I'll never have statues or other memorials built in my memory. I'm not going to be famous like them."

I disagree with that kind of thinking. You have no idea how God might choose to use you or your children or your children's children. You must understand that God's Word gives us the foundation from which we can do our best to build the right structure in our families. God's Word (not your own wisdom or strength) is the basis of a godly legacy. The Bible alone is living and active, and able to divide and judge correctly, and its principles can lead to astounding results.

If you are going to leave a legacy like Bunyan or Luther, you are going to have to decide to go against the flow because the flow of the world today is leading to decay, death, and even hell. Each of us has a personal choice to make regarding the future of our family. Will we lead into a legacy of life and freedom based on the Word of God, or will we lead our families into a legacy of relativism and death, as did Darwin?

The question is not rhetorical, but immensely practical, affecting everything that you might do and everything you might be. The type of legacy you choose will most likely have great impact on your community, your world, and, most graphically, your family. Which will it be? Will you lead your family into a legacy of truth, life, and freedom based on the Word of God, or will you lead your family into a legacy of relativism, bondage, and death, as did Darwin? It's a decision each one of us must make. I know, I had to do it myself, and it was a critical decision in my ongoing journey for truth and answers.

When I started high school, I eagerly looked forward to my science lessons. However, I was perplexed when the teacher taught that humans evolved from "ape-men" and that animals had evolved over millions of years. My textbooks laid out what claimed to be convincing proof that we progressed from molecules to man without any outside influence. I was further taught ideas on how the universe had formed — but they all involved naturalistic processes. God wasn't involved at all. They claimed that everything somehow "exploded" out of nothing all by itself, and they made it all sound so "scientific." Everything I was taught about the origin of matter, life, and man conflicted with what my parents had taught me from the Bible. How was I to resolve this?

I sat down with my father and asked him to help me sort this out. Sadly, at that time there were no books or other resources that we were aware of that dealt with the creation/evolution issue. Certainly, none were readily available to us in Australia at that time. (When I look at all the resources available today, I often think back to this time in my life and realize how blessed people are today.)

From a scientific perspective, my father didn't have the scientific answers to the supposed ape-men fossils, or the billions of years of evolution, or the supposed "big bang" history of the universe. He wasn't a scientist, and he didn't understand where these ideas had come from. Now my father did have lots of answers to show how these secular ideas contradicted Scripture. He explained that if the origins account in Genesis wasn't literal history, then there was no foundation for marriage, for the gospel — for any doctrine. I recognized we had to search for and wait for answers in the science area. But I knew we would not reinterpret God's Word to fit with man's beliefs about origins.

I completed high school, rejecting mole-cules-to-man evolution as a philosophy, but I still didn't have any solid scientific answers to defend my position. I was concerned about this, but my father's words kept ringing in my ears: *Even if we can't find an answer to explain why the secular idea is wrong, we need to continue to search and wait for the answer.*

During my college years while studying for my science degree, I was bombarded with evolutionary ideas in biology, geology, and other subject areas. I still had no scientific response to what I was being taught, so I just lived with the dilemma — though I recognized that sooner or later I had to sort this out in some way. As I studied, however, I did observe that my textbooks and professors did not have con-vincing evidence for Darwinian evolution or the supposed billions of years for the age of the earth. I recognized there were numerous assumptions behind the various interpretations of fossil bones and the supposed long ages attributed to them, but I really wanted some definitive answers.

A little booklet that dealt with the creation/evolution issue from a biblical perspective came into my possession.

As I read through this booklet, one particular section stood out from all the others. The author stated that from a biblical perspective, there could not have been death, disease, and bloodshed of animals and man before sin, since this would destroy the foundations of the gospel. As I thought about this, something really hit me between the eyes: A Christian can't consistently accept the idea of an earth that is billions of years old (with its supposed millions of years of layers of fossils that we know contain evidence of cancer and other diseases in bones) and accept the statements concerning sin and death in the Bible. Over the years, we have certainly developed such arguments to a much more sophisticated level, but the respect I had for the authority of the Word as instilled in me by my father caused me to recognize the vital importance of this death issue.

This small booklet gave me a number of biblical arguments about why Christians can't accept molecules-to-man evolution and the Bible's record of origins at the same time. For example, Darwinian evolution teaches man evolved from ape-like ancestors, but the Bible teaches Adam was created from dust and Eve was created from his side (Paul in 1 Corinthians 11:8 states woman was made from man). Thus, there is no way one can consistently reconcile the Genesis account of the creation of man (if one takes it at face value) with the Darwinian account. These explanations sustained me for some time.

As the years progressed, the Lord confirmed in my thinking that it was important to wait for answers, just as my father had trained me. I learned to continue in heartfelt faith, based on what God said in His Word, in spite of a lack of understanding. Passages from Job have helped me considerably in dealing with secular ideas and secular interpretations of evidence when they conflict with what the Word of God says: "Where were you when I laid the foundation of the earth? Tell me, if you have understanding" (Job 38:4).

> Then Job answered the LORD and said:
> "I know that you can do all things, and that no

purpose of yours can be thwarted. 'Who is this that hides counsel without knowledge?' Therefore I have uttered what I did not understand, things too wonderful for me, which I did not know. 'Hear, and I will speak; I will question you, and you make it known to me.' I had heard of you by the hearing of the ear, but now my eye sees you; therefore I despise myself, and repent in dust and ashes" (Job 42:1–6).

God aggressively quizzes Job through chapters 38 to 42, asking him questions about various animals and other aspects of the earth and universe that Job cannot possibly answer. "Job, were you there when I made the earth? Do you know this? What about this, Job? Do you understand that? How much do you know about this?" At the end of God's inquisition, Job falls down in dust and ashes, basically saying, "I give up Lord — compared to you I know nothing." My father reminded me many times that God is infinite in knowledge and wisdom, and so we know basically nothing compared to God. How dare we as fallible humans take our fallible ideas to God's Word and reinterpret it!

Psalm 147:5 reminds us that "Great is our Lord, and abundant in power; his understanding is beyond measure." It is absolutely impossible that we should understand everything . . . yet God does, and for the time being, He has given us all the answers we need for a big-picture understanding of life and the universe in His holy and perfect Bible.

My father's words echoed the truth of the Job passages. To this day, I often remember one of the things my father taught me: if the Bible can't be trusted in one area, how can it be trusted anywhere else? Dad clearly understood the importance of not compromising God's Word with man's fallible ideas . . . and he taught me to do the same. Looking back on this time, I can't help but think of Proverbs 2:3–6:

> Yes, if you call out for insight and raise your
> voice for understanding, if you seek it like
> silver and search for it as for hidden treasures,
> then you will understand the fear of the LORD
> and find the knowledge of God. For the LORD
> gives wisdom; from his mouth come knowl-
> edge and understanding.

So, as I prayed for answers, I held to my faith in a vacuum of scientific evidence. Still, I felt the conflict between what many called "science" and my faith. (I found out later that there is a big difference between "observational science" which we all agree with, and "historical science" which involves the scientist's beliefs about the past.) I really wanted to honor God's Word and find the answers that would confirm what I believed to be true. After all, if God's account of origins is true, then observational science should confirm that — and today we know it overwhelmingly does. I wanted some scientific answers to sort this out, but where would I find them? While I didn't know it at the time, God was working in a special way to provide them for me.

God heard my earnest prayers. In 1974, during my post-graduate year, I mentioned the creation/ evolution issue and my dilemma to a friend. He told me about a book that had been published in America which gave lots of scientific answers concerning geology and Noah's Flood. Where would I obtain such a book? I traveled into the city of Brisbane to visit the only Christian bookstore I was aware of. It was on the second floor of an old building — not very easy to find. When

I described this book on the Flood to the woman looking after the store, she immediately went and found a copy of *The Genesis Flood* by the late Drs. Morris and Whitcomb. (I still have this first major creation book that began my creation library.)

As I read the book, I found so many answers to questions about dating methods, rock layers, fossils, and many other aspects of the creation/evolution issue. I was so excited! They were answers that made sense and clearly showed that observational science confirmed the Bible's account of creation and the Flood. (Even though some of the arguments in this book are now out of date, subsequent research built on this publication has only reinforced the overwhelming evidence that confirms the Bible's account of history in Genesis.) My eyes were opened, and I began to understand the nature of the scientific arguments concerning the origins issue for the first time. I clearly remember smiling and thinking, *Once again my father's stand on the Scripture has been vindicated — and once again God's infallible Word has judged the pretense of the evolutionists and the compromise of liberal theologians.*

Almost 30 years later, while visiting a particular tourist attraction in Brisbane, an elderly lady recognized me and approached me. As we talked, I realized that she and her husband had owned the Christian bookstore where I purchased *The Genesis Flood*. I explained to her that this was the first major creation apologetics book I had obtained and that it was an integral part of my journey through life. I shared with her that the Lord used that book, and the other booklet I had read, to begin a biblical creation apologetics ministry in Australia, then Answers in Genesis in the United States, and now many other parts of the world. This also led to the construction of the two leading Christian-themed attractions in the world, the Creation Museum and the Ark Encounter.

She became very excited and told me that her husband had had a real interest in science, the Bible, and the creation/evolution issue. He had such a burden from the Lord, that he made sure he had a copy of *The Genesis Flood* in his bookshop after he found out about it. That book was there on the shelf waiting for me to purchase it. God sovereignly orchestrated this so I would be able to obtain this publication.

Soon, I took the book to my father, saying, "Dad, I've found many more answers to the creation/evolution/age of earth issues! Observational science does confirm the Genesis account!" To this day, I can still picture that smile on his face as he flipped through the pages. He so loved the Word of God and was so thrilled to have adequate answers to uphold God's Word in Genesis. If my father had compromised his stand on the Word before he had the evidence to confirm its authority, I don't believe I would be writing this book or be involved in active ministry today. Thankfully, my father's faith held, and he chose to act on it. In the process, he began a legacy of worldwide influence that neither of us dreamed possible — not from a no-name bunch of outback Australians at least!

****

In a public cemetery in the city of Brisbane, Australia, stands a particular gravestone. The marker is not outstanding in any sense; it is not in any prominent place, nor do tourists gather at this spot. Throughout the city of Brisbane there are neither statues nor memorials in memory of the man whose body rests below the marker.

As one among the thousands of other gravestones, this marker is not easy to find. Unless you were specifically looking for it, there would be no reason to even think about searching for it or to think it should be noteworthy from all the others, but it is noteworthy to me — even more than those

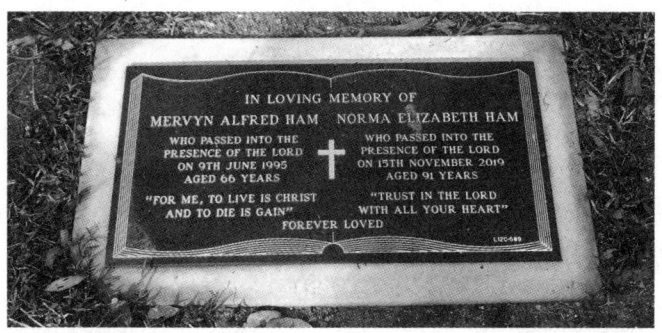

of Luther and Bunyan. The words on this gravestone are few and simple:

> In loving memory of Mervyn Alfred Ham
> who passed into the presence of the Lord
> on 9th June 1995
> Aged 66 years
> "For me to live is Christ and to die is gain"
> Forever loved

No signs, no statues, no museum. Some of the graves in this cemetery have massive structures to bring attention to them.

And at the same gravesite 24 years later, we read on the gravestone along with my Dad's memorial:

> In loving memory of
> Norma Elizabeth Ham
> who passed into the

presence of the Lord
on 15th November 2019
Aged 91 years
"Trust in the Lord with all your heart"
Forever loved

My dad, together with my precious and godly mother, will be remembered by memorials of a different kind . . . memorials that will stand into eternity, long after the plaques and portraits of others have fallen. Mum and Dad produced six living memorials in their children, and we, in turn, are now creating a godly inheritance to leave to our children. By the grace of God, it will be a godly legacy that will teach and remind people for generations about the authority of the Word of God and the saving mercy of our Lord Jesus Christ. That's what the family was meant to do — produce godly offspring who will marry godly offspring and produce godly offspring generation after generation.

A rag-tag bunch we are, dented and tainted by our own sin. We all have our struggles and battles with the old nature, but we praise the Lord for the godly parents to whom we were entrusted to be trained for our ministries in this world and the next.

Understanding the sovereignty of God, I know I would not be in this ministry if it wasn't for the upbringing my parents gave me. They set the example as dedicated and humble Christians who intentionally sought to raise a godly family that would evangelize the lost in an ungodly world. The Answers in Genesis ministry is itself a memorial to my parents and the legacy they began in my life and in the world.

Please understand that you too will leave a legacy to the generations to follow. They may not build memorials to you, and it's unlikely that they will place signs outside of the place of your birth . . . but what you leave behind will forever impact the hearts and souls of those in your family and beyond. You will leave a legacy; the only question is what kind of legacy it will be. May you recognize from this day forward one certain thing: The foundation of a legacy worth leaving is made up of a faith in God, and a trust in His Holy Word. All we have to build will either stand or fall on this foundation. Think about your children, grandchildren, and great-grandchildren — will they stand as warriors for the Lord? Or will they succumb to the giants because of lack of training?

Consider this question: What will your children say about you when you die? When your days are done, what kind of legacy will live on in those you touched? Most importantly, will the Lord say, "Well done, good and faithful servant" (Matthew 25:21)? "Be faithful unto death, and I will give you the crown of life" (Revelation 2:10).

Key thoughts from this chapter:

1. Everyone leaves a legacy. The only question is what kind of legacy it will be.

2. A godly legacy is built on the authority and sufficiency of the Bible.

3. A godly legacy begins with a decision and may require waiting for answers to certain questions.

4. Leaving a legacy is a big deal. Our children, grandchildren, and the world will be eternally impacted by it.

GODLY

GENERATIONS

∾

When I was growing up, a group of people intentionally removed themselves from the modern world and disappeared into the jungles of the Northern Tropics of Australia. Seeking a liberated and simple existence, free from the pressures and constraints of the world, they left behind their past identity and heritage, shedding their inhibitions (and most of their clothes!). They were known as the "hippies," and their offspring were not familiar with modern medicines or technology. They had little or no respect for society's laws, and many of their children received no formal education. Concepts like "god" and "truth" were not considered important enough to teach. Consequentially, and tragically, they basically degenerated into a non-God-fearing and a non-technological culture in one generation. In less than two decades, they produced a new generation, by and large ignorant of their former heritage and culture — in a sense, we could say it was a "primitive culture."

The lesson is clear: If we don't transmit our knowledge of God to the next generation, it will be lost. Those that follow may not have any means of regaining it, and they probably won't even be aware of the need to do so. This has happened in the past to the New Guinea natives, the American Indians, the North Africans, and many others. All are descendants of Adam, yet somewhere in their past, fathers did not pass on the knowledge they had regarding God and their origins. Thus, when discovered by the Europeans, they were regarded as "primitive."

When the Europeans first discovered the Australian Aboriginal people, they too were an anti-God, spiritist culture. Do you realize that, in reality, it could have taken only one generation to produce such a culture? Like us, the Australian Aboriginals had an ancestor who knew all about the true God . . . and he could even build ships! His name was Noah. At some point in history, the ancestors of today's Aboriginal people did not transmit the true knowledge of God or the technology they once had to their offspring, and their godly legacy was lost.

It's fascinating to note that the Australian Aborigines had legends which sound like parts of Genesis 1–11. They had legends about a flood that are quite similar to the account of Noah's Flood in Genesis 6 through 9. They also had creation legends that exhibited many similarities with the biblical account of Adam and Eve and the entrance of sin and death after Adam took the fruit. (This is strong circumstantial evidence that the Australian Aborigines are descendants of Noah.) After the Tower of Babel, as people groups split up and spread throughout the earth, many transmitted the history of their ancestors to coming generations. The account of the Flood was handed down, but the details changed over the years as it was passed on verbally, rather than in written form, as were the Scriptures. In the Aboriginal legends, just as in the "Flood legends" of many other cultures, there are many elements similar to the Bible's account, which is the original and accurately recorded written account that has not been changed.

Sadly, however, the Australian Aboriginals (as well as many other cultures) lost almost all of the knowledge they once had. I'll never forget visiting an Aboriginal mission station in North Queensland and hearing the story of an Aboriginal elder. The elder said he remembered wandering with his father as nomads across the Australian deserts. He asked his father, "What is God like?" His father replied, "I don't know, son. We've forgotten."

What a tragedy. The knowledge of God was not transmitted to the next generation — and now it was all but gone. When I spoke to the Australian Aboriginal students in my classes, in essence, I was re-establishing the right foundation of thinking that had been lost for many generations.

Numerous examples from biblical history also reveal that a legacy can be lost in one generation. For example, the Bible makes it clear that Ham committed some serious sin in regard to his father. Ham's youngest son, Canaan, also had some serious problems in his life, serious enough that Noah said, "Cursed be Canaan!" (Genesis 9:25). When one looks at the descendants of Canaan, we see the people of Sodom, Gomorrah, and the Canaanites — some of the most wicked people who lived on earth.

It certainly appears that Ham did not train Canaan effectively. Most likely, the same sin in Ham existed in Canaan — but to a greater extent, which often happens to the next generation. (When a particular sin in one generation is not dealt with, the same sin is often seen in subsequent generations but to an even greater extent.)

Another example of the devastation of generational compromise is found in the Books of Kings and Chronicles. As you read through Kings, you are able to see the great degree of love and devotion that both David and Solomon had for God. Both kings — father and son — had a strong focus on the worship of the one true God alone. David, in particular, was uncompromising. Their devotion was demonstrated in their desire and commitment to build the great temple of the Lord. We read in Acts 13:22 that ". . . he raised up David to be their king, of whom he testified and said, 'I have found in David the son of Jesse a man after my heart, who will do all my will.'"

Devastation, however, comes all too easily. Solomon's compromise started with him having many wives and allowing them to worship their pagan gods. Then he allowed these pagan influences to infiltrate his people, resulting in them worshiping the foreign gods as well (1 Kings 11:1–4). Within one generation, Solomon's son Rehoboam made a compromising allowance for people who wanted to partake in the same idol worship in the high places. From then on, Judah spiraled further into compromise and wickedness (1 Kings 14:23). In the generation after Rehoboam, King Asa inherited the evil idolatry already in place from the previous two generations.

He was a "good" king, but he lacked the instruction and wisdom to eradicate this evil (1 Kings 15:11–15). The next generation was then even more distant from acknowledging this great compromise.

The compromise of Solomon and his failure to teach and lead the next generation led to a blatant disregard for God's Word. Israel had been clearly instructed not to have any gods above the one true God. Solomon's failure had disastrous effects on the worship of an entire nation for generations to come. From then on, a consistent theme runs through the Book of Kings as we read time and time again that each king continued to allow worship of foreign gods in the "high places."

Finally, at the end of 2 Kings, King Josiah rediscovered God's Word and dealt decisively with the abomination of the high places. After reading about the many consequences of ignoring God's instruction and the many warnings from godly prophets about further future consequences, King Josiah again brought Judah's focus back to the one true God alone (2 Kings 23:4–14). It is true that God was never going to be unfaithful to His commitment to Israel as His chosen people, but God did not ignore His people disregarding His instruction. A deviation of commitment to God's

Word resulted in devastating consequences both for Israel and Judah for generations.

This is the overwhelmingly clear message to all of us: Humanity has never been, and never will be, able to disregard the written Word of God without major generational consequences. Oh, how I groan in my spirit today as I see the consequences of a lukewarm compromising church throughout the land — through the entire Western world. As in the days of King Josiah, we need a new reformation today to return to the authority of the Word of God. And this must begin in our homes and churches.

Lost generations can only be restored when God's Word is again accepted uncompromisingly as truth.

The consequences of an ungodly legacy are incalculable. The repercussions send shock waves into the next generation, and even into eternity. That's why our first "component for a godly legacy" is a compelling conviction that leads us to prioritize training up a godly generation.

My Journey with Mally

When I was around ten years old, my parents hosted a missionary from Open Air Campaigners who was running a series of programs for adults and children at a nearby church. My parents widely advertised these programs and encouraged people to attend. I distinctly remember Dad and Mum picking up as many children as they could fit into the car to take them to these special outreaches. One night, I remember God instilling in me for the first time the conviction to devote my life to passing the Word of God on to the next generations.

During one of the sessions for young people, the speaker challenged us to make a decision to be a missionary for the Lord. I'll never forget the strong conviction I had to make that decision. I met with the missionary after the meeting along with a number of others. We even signed a written declaration of what we had done. We prayed and made this very sincere commitment. I didn't know that this would mean that some 25 years later my wife and I would heed the call to leave our homeland and move to the United States as missionaries to challenge the American culture and call the church back to its foundation of the authority of the Word of God.

Like me, Mally was sent to Sunday school by her parents. One Sunday the teacher challenged the children to come forward to give their lives to the Lord. Mally knew that God had done so much for her by sending His Son to die on a Cross to save her. In her heart she prayed, "Lord if you did that for me, dying on the Cross, I want to go anywhere and do anything you want me to do." Being very shy, she told God that she would only go forward if someone else went forward, too. When she looked up, she saw that the whole Sunday school class had gone forward!

When Mally and I worked out the date this would have occurred, it was at much the same time as when I told the Lord I was willing to be a missionary for Him. The Lord was preparing both of us for a road ahead together . . . yet we had no inclination at the time that the other even existed. What a sovereign God we have! Little did we know what would be in store for us as the Lord took us up on our promise to serve Him!

The first time I did lay eyes on Mally, I really think it was "love at first sight." (For me, at least; Mally may have had her doubts!) In January 1971, I walked into our new church in Brisbane and was handed a hymn book by this young lady welcoming people at the door. I took the book, and she took my heart and has never given me reason to want it back. Mally too will tell you that there was something special about that first meeting, but it took some time before I captured her heart. We began meeting each other on a regular basis, and in March 1972, we were engaged. We exchanged our wedding vows on December 30, 1972.

I was married to a wonderful Christian wife.

In 1976, during my second year of teaching, our first child, Nathan Robert Ham, was born in the country town of Dalby. Suddenly, we were parents. As I held that baby in my arms and looked into his face, I knew that my life had new focus and purpose.

We wanted to serve the Lord to the utmost of our abilities. We were actively involved in the local church, and of course I was a "creation activist" at the local high school. Having my own son now, I felt profoundly different. As I replayed memories of my own childhood in my mind, thinking of how my father had invested his life in me, I began to ponder how to train up this child — the first of the next generation of Hams. What methods should we use? How could we make sure we did our best to

The day our firstborn was dedicated in church in Dalby, Queensland, by pastor Jim Kitson

see our children become committed Christians like ourselves? How do we ensure the biblical legacy that we have inherited continues?

As new parents, we thought long and hard about what we should do to ensure we were bringing up our children in the correct way. Again, remembering how I learned as a child to build my thinking on the Scriptures, we began to develop a Christian worldview in child training, one based on the Bible . . . just as my father had done before me.

Reasons for the Family

The family is the first and most fundamental of all human institutions ordained in Scripture. We praise the Lord that we were brought up in a Christian family with godly parents, knowing that many others haven't had this gift. Our faults were (and are) many, but I've often felt that our family is entrusted with a special inheritance that we need to share with others . . . and so is yours.

The family is the backbone of a nation.

God uses the family unit to transmit His knowledge from one generation to the next and be "salt" and "light" in the world. If the family can be destroyed, the Christian fabric in society will ultimately unravel.

The family was first ordained when God created a helper suitable for man and instructed them to be "fruitful and multiply" (Genesis 1:28). Like so many other essential doctrines of the Christian faith, the origin of marriage (and thus the family unit) finds its beginning in the Book of Genesis. Think about it: If the first 11 chapters of Genesis are not literally true, then the teaching on the family has no literal historical basis, and thus a family could be anything you wish to make it, but that is not the case. Evidence shows that the Genesis origin of the family is credible and historical.

For example, Jesus Christ quoted from Genesis chapters 1 and 2 to give the foundation of marriage and thus proclaim the true meaning of marriage. We read in Matthew 19:4–5 (and also Mark 10) when Jesus was asked about marriage:

> He answered, "Have you not read that he who created them from the beginning made them male and female, and said, 'Therefore a man shall leave his father and his mother and hold fast to his wife, and the two shall become one flesh'?"

The above passage is a reference to the creation of male and female (Genesis 1:27) and that Adam and

Eve were one flesh as woman was made from man (Genesis 2:24) — thus the two become one physically (and spiritually).

The origin of marriage is in Genesis. And it is to be one man (male) and one woman (female). There's no such thing as gay "marriage," as marriage is a God-ordained institution (they need to call it gay union or something like that!). In today's world, you and your children will hear that marriage can be two men or two women as long as they love each other. But that's not what God's Word states. The LGBTQ movement and the promotion of gay "marriage" and transgender is one of the greatest attacks on the family today. It's a big part of the war against children and the war against the family. Satan knows if he can destroy the family unit, then he destroys the backbone of the culture and destroys the most fundamental of all human institutions God ordained to produce godly offspring and impact the world for Christ generation after generation.

As an example of the war against the family, an article in the *Journal of Medical Ethics*[1] and reported

---

1. Samuel Dubin et al., "Medically assisted gender affirmation: when children and parents disagree," *Journal of Medical Ethics* (2019), https://jme.bmj.com/content/early/2019/12/31/medethics-2019-105567.

on in the news media,[2] suggested children could be taken away from their parents if they oppose sex change surgeries and hormone therapy. Now God makes it clear in His Word that He has ordained the government for the role of maintaining law and order (Romans 13). The government has stepped in to so many other areas now to control morality, marriage, and the training of children. Parents, not the government, are given (by God) the role of training children (e.g., Ephesians 6:4)! But in a culture that increasingly rejects God's Word, we see the government infringing on the rights of parents to control the coming generations. The government doesn't own our children — God does. And He has given parents the responsibility of raising them up to be godly offspring (e.g., Malachi 2:15).

The authority Christ gives for the family is the origins account in Genesis. Jesus created "all things" (Colossians 1:16). In Him "are hidden all the treasures of wisdom and knowledge" (Colossians 2:3). He is "the truth" (John 14:6), and He is

2. Jonathan Van Maren, "*Journal of Medical Ethics* suggests children could be taken away from their parents if they oppose sex change surgeries and hormone therapy" (*The Bridgehead*, February 3, 2020), accessed May 6, 2020, https://thebridgehead.ca/2020/02/03/journal-of-medical-ethics-suggests-children-could-be-taken-away-from-their-parents-if-they-oppose-sex-change-surgeries-and-hormone-therapy.

"the Word" (John 1:1). Jesus' authority is clear, and His recognition of the authority and origin of the Genesis family is significant. The Apostle Paul did much the same in Ephesians 5.

Obviously, Jesus would not quote a myth as the foundation of marriage. To do so would make marriage mean whatever you wanted it to mean, with the added consequences that Jesus would not be the truth and the Bible would not be infallible. This is discussed in detail in various creation apologetics books and articles.

Note also that God ordained only one kind of family — a female mother and a male father. Mark 10:6–7 states, "But from the beginning of creation, 'God made them male and female.' 'Therefore a man shall leave his father and mother and hold fast to his wife.'" Again, the reference to Genesis 1 and 2.

What then is the reason for marriage? What is its primary importance? Why did God make two "become one" (Genesis 2:24)? Procreation (having children) is certainly a part of the scriptural mandate that God has given to parents and must be considered as one of the primary important reasons for marriage. (I do understand that in a sin-cursed world, some couples sadly can't have biological children). With five kids of our own (and now 17 grandchildren!), I can honestly say that my wife and I have done our part to fulfill this mandate to "go forth and multiply"! This does not seem to be the norm in our culture anymore, however.

In 1986, my wife and our four Australian children (our fifth was born in San Diego in 1988) arrived on a Qantas flight into Los Angeles.

As we stood up to leave the plane, someone yelled out, "Man, what a troop!" It was as if we were out of the ordinary because we had four children. In this age, many married couples are deciding to have none, one, or only a couple of children. With four, we were considered unusual. However, families with many children are becoming more common again, particularly within the homeschool movement and other groups within the culture. I meet homeschool families these days with seven, eight, and even a dozen children — I wonder what that person on the plane would have said if he had seen one of these families!

Certainly, the Scripture doesn't dictate how many children a couple should have and there can be many reasons — whether medical or other — why some couples might have few or no children.

Coming to America

However, we should all be at least aware that one of the primary purposes for marriage has not changed — to produce offspring. We certainly need to make sure we don't have a self-centered attitude when considering such matters.

It is significant that Scripture is even more specific than telling us to just have offspring; we are commanded to have godly offspring. In Malachi 2:15, the prophet was condemning the Israelite men for taking pagan wives: "Did he not make them one, with a portion of the Spirit in their union? And what was the one God seeking? Godly offspring. So guard yourselves in your spirit, and let none of you be faithless to the wife of your youth."

This passage answers the "Why marriage?" question directly. Why does God make two people one flesh? What is this all about? From your union he seeks "godly offspring." One of the primary reasons for marriage is to produce godly children; it is not just "offspring" you are to produce, but "godly offspring." Certainly, there are other purposes for this union of man and woman, but a primary purpose for this union called marriage, which is binding and established by God in Genesis, is to have godly seed.

If we don't produce godly offspring, how will the future generations of the world hear the truth about living a righteous life? Romans 10:14 puts it to us this way: "How then will they call on him in whom they have not believed? And how are they to believe in him of whom they have never heard? And how are they to hear without someone preaching?"

If godly offspring are not being produced as they used to be to a much greater degree (as statistics indicate in our once-Christianized West), could our culture end up spiritually vacant like the Australian Aboriginals, or the American Indians? Not only could it happen, but in many parts of our culture and our world, it is happening. We have to look no further than Europe to see that the peoples who were once at the center of Christian strength have now become almost entirely void of the things of God.

Note the following graph.[3]

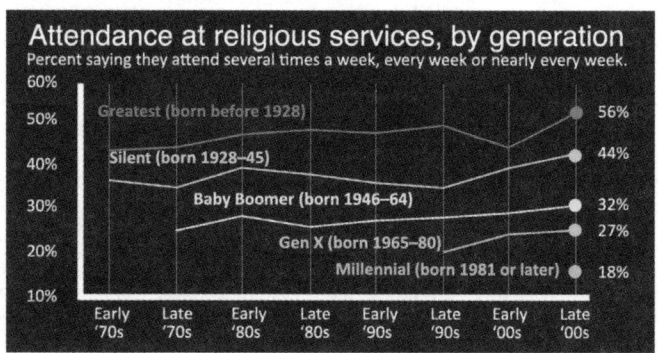

Attendance at religious services, by generation
Percent saying they attend several times a week, every week or nearly every week.

Greatest (born before 1928) — 56%
Silent (born 1928–45) — 44%
Baby Boomer (born 1946–64) — 32%
Gen X (born 1965–80) — 27%
Millennial (born 1981 or later) — 18%

Church attendance in the USA (some statistics now show Millennial church attendance as low as 11%.)

Generation Z in the USA are twice as likely to be atheist as any previous generation.

3. Pew Research Center, "Religion Among the Millennials," A Pew Forum on Religion & Public Life Report, February 2010, 7.

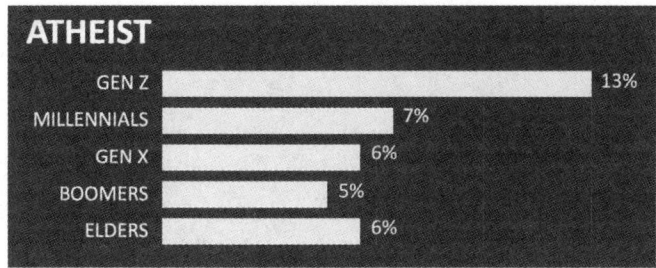

At the time of writing this, not a lot of research has been done on Generation Z,[4] as they are the youngest group. But indications are that regular church attendance from this group will end up being less than the millennials. Take into account these figures from Barna about Generation Z:[5]

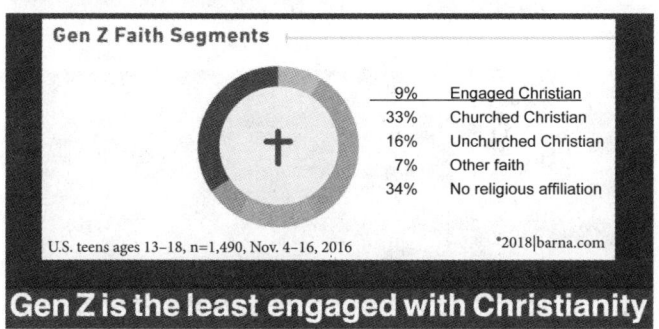

Gen Z is the least engaged with Christianity

4. "Atheism Doubles Among Generation Z," Barna, January 24, 2018, https://www.barna.com/research/atheism-doubles-among-generation-z/.
5. *Gen Z: The Culture, Beliefs and Motivations Shaping the Next Generation*, Barna Group Report Produced in Partnership with Impact 360 Institute, 2018.

What about Gen Z?

The percentage of people with a biblical worldview declines in each generation.

Boomers—10%   Gen X—7%   Millennials—6%

Gen Z—4%

Church attendance in the United Kingdom:[6, 7]

5.4% of the English population attends church on a given Sunday, with only 3.5% of 15–19 year olds and 5.9% of 20–29 year olds.

Church attendance in Britain
1980–2015

England has the lowest percentage of the population attending church in 2015 (4.7%), just below Wales at 4.8%. In Scotland, the equivalent figure is 8.9%.

---

6. Peter Brierley ed., "Introduction: UK Church Statistics No 3: 2018 Edition," *Brierley Consultancy*, No 3: 2018 Edition, ADBC Publishers.
7. "Christianity in the UK," Faith Survey, August 13, 2018, https://faithsurvey.co.uk/uk-christianity.htmI.

Study the extent of these worldview attitudes in the UK/Europe:[8]

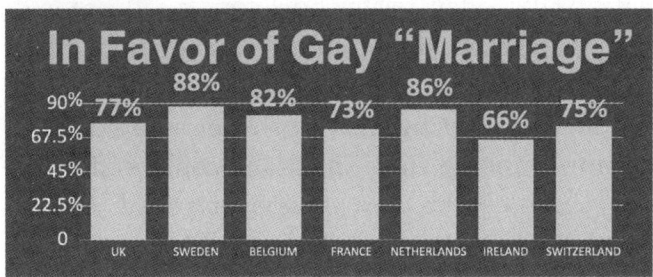

Now I could include pages and pages of statistics — but it's best to sum them up this way. The Western world used to have a considerably dominant Christianized worldview, but this has dramatically changed. Now the Western world has become very secularized, and there has been an exodus from the church each subsequent generation. As generations X, Y, and Z become the dominant groups in the culture, we will see catastrophic change in the culture morally and in many other ways. We've seen this in many ways already, but I suggest that's nothing compared to what's coming if it continues

8. "Eastern and Western Europeans Differ on Importance of Religion, Views of Minorities, and Key Social Issues," Pew Research Center, October 29, 2018, https://www.pewforum. org/2018/10/29/eastern-and-western-europeans-differ-on-importance-of-religion-views-of-minorities-and-key-social-issues/.

the way it is. Why has this happened? I believe much of the blame lies with families and the church! My wife, Mally, often relates how concerned she is in regard to what sort of culture our grandchildren will be living in! The growing intolerance of any semblance of a Christian worldview should shock us into thinking that Christians could suffer real persecution in the West as we've only read about in *Foxe's Book of Martyrs* or Hebrews 11.

We must produce godly offspring who, in turn, will transmit the knowledge they have to the next generation so they will be able to transmit this to the following generation — generation after generation. It is a strategic and eternally vital task, and it obviously requires considerable work to ensure information is passed on and not lost from succeeding generations. Every generation has to face "giants," as those on the broad way who come against Christians can seem to be so powerful and overwhelming. But those who have been trained to stand on God's Word and are equipped to defend the faith will have the courage and ability to face these "giants."

Training That Matters

As Mally and I looked at our new son and pondered how to raise him in the things of the Lord, we were convicted by a question which has helped us develop a biblical view for bringing up our children. We challenge you to think about this question, too: *Knowing that God is the only One who knows everything and who made all things, and believing that the Bible is His Word, what does God say about training children — the methods, the priorities, the nature of children, how to discipline them, etc.?*

If you can't answer that question, then let me ask you another question in blunt English: Why are you having children if you don't know what God's Word teaches concerning how to raise them? And therefore, whose methods are you using then? You might know what psychologists, pastors, or your parents say, but do you know what God says in His Word?

As an itinerant speaker, it is easy for me to ask pointed questions like this because I usually don't know the parents in the audience at all. It's much harder for the pastor to ask those questions because he often already knows the answer, and the parents in the church know that he knows the answer, and they all know that they have to live with each other! That is why it is much easier for itinerant speakers to get away with challenging audiences in such matters, plus it's safer! I can stir them up and then get on a plane the next morning, leaving the pastor to deal with the controversy!

Sadly, from my experience traveling around Australia, the United Kingdom, and the United States, there are increasing numbers of Christian parents who are not using God's methods to produce godly offspring. On top of that, many parents don't know what the standards are by which to judge their children's behavior, so they don't know if their children measure up to godly standards. Because standards have generally dropped, many cannot see the ungodly behavior or attitudes of their offspring — they can't even recognize it. Television is a prime example. What would have been called "obscene" on television a generation ago is the norm today, and Christian parents rarely censor these programs.

Why is this so? What has happened to cause this situation? In many ways, we can use the old analogy of the "cold-blooded toad." Because a toad does not maintain a constant body temperature like a mammal, supposedly, so the story goes, you can put it in cold water and heat it up so that the toad really does not recognize that it is being boiled to death until it is too late. Regardless of whether that will really happen, we have become like that toad.

We have lowered our standards to accommodate the world around us little by little, and now we can't see how much we have deviated from the standards we used to keep and should still be keeping if they are grounded in God's Word.[9]

The lack of a solidly biblical approach in the area of the family and education has done great harm to an entire generation of Christian children — and we are suffering the consequences in a big way. The time not spent by a father training just one child can lead to hundreds, or thousands, or millions not having the knowledge of God. (Remember the descendants of Canaan?!)

If you are a parent reading this book, do you really think you have built your thinking about child training on Scripture? Are you doing your best to train up your children to be godly offspring as the Scripture outlines for us? Could you write down clear biblical guidelines for raising your children?

Think carefully about that last question. Why not take pen and paper and see if you can answer it? If we are truly Christians and understand that our thinking must be built on the infallible Word of

9. The boiling frog anecdote has been challenged in recent times; however, the principle remains the same. http://www.answersingenesis.org/articles/rgc/godly-generations#fnList_1_1.

God, then we should be able to write down all that God tells us about training children.

Each time I give my presentation on the family, I ask the audience to think over whether or not they could write down these things. When I do, a quiet hush comes over the auditorium because the majority of Christian parents cannot do this! The same question can be asked of Christian teachers, Sunday school teachers, pastors, etc. If we cannot write down what God says about training children, then what right do we have to teach children or bring them into the world or make decisions or recommendations concerning their education?

Husbands and wives have all sorts of opinions about what a family is supposed to be, and all sorts of opinions about how to train children. But it is not a matter of our opinion; it is what God instructs us to do that matters. My wife and I have searched the Scriptures to obtain God's instructions and then apply them in our family. We certainly do not have all the answers, but together we have diligently sought to use the revealed Word of God as the basis for our thinking. Our children are far from perfect and are certainly a constant source of blessings and challenges. However, we are proud parents of children who want to love and obey the Lord Jesus

Christ with all their hearts. And what a blessing to see them now doing their best to raise up godly off-spring. I am writing these pages to share with you just some of the highlights of what we have found from the Scriptures that we apply in our family daily to attempt to fulfill Proverbs 22:6: "Train up a child in the way he should go; even when he is old he will not depart from it."

Poodles and Priorities

I have another question I like to ask my audiences: "What are you taking to heaven with you?" Most initially respond by saying, "Nothing!" That's almost right. You certainly can't take your bank account, your car, home, or boat, but you can take your chil-dren with you. If you are willing and committed, God can use you as a vehicle to help transport your children to heaven . . . but you have to take it seri-ously. Look at the picture on the following page and then answer yet another question: Which one of these will last forever?

We know that the car, boat, house, and money will all perish. What about the poodle? Sometimes children ask me if their pet dog or cat will be in heaven. I usually say, "Well, if your pet is needed in heaven, I'm sure God will make sure it is there."

I know that's dodging the issue, but it's the nicest way I can think of to tell people that I don't believe animals continue to live on after death. Ecclesiastes 3:21 seems to hint that animals do not have immortal souls when it asks, "Who knows if the human spirit rises upward and if the spirit of the animal goes down into the earth?" (NIV). On top of that, animals were not made in the image of God, whereas humans were. So, of all the things in the picture, only the soul of the child is going to last forever.

Now observe the next picture and answer this question. Which one of these can you take with you to heaven?

The answer is obvious — only the child can be taken to heaven.

Parents, think about this: Every child conceived in a mother's womb is a conscious being who is going to live forever and ever and ever and ever and ever and ever — in either heaven or hell. Does that tell you something about what your priorities should be in regard to time and money? Consider this as you read Philippians 3:7–8:

> But whatever gain I had, I counted as loss for the sake of Christ. Indeed, I count everything as loss because of the surpassing worth of knowing Christ Jesus my Lord. For his sake I have suffered the loss of all things and count them as rubbish, in order that I may gain Christ.

The most important thing for anyone is that they know Christ. Nothing else ultimately matters in the big picture of things. Our lives on this earth are so short — in fact, they add up to nothing compared to eternity. The car, the house, the career . . . all will vanish with time, but the soul of your child will live forever. Doesn't that make you want to take a serious look at how you are bringing up your children? Jeremiah 9:23–24 reminds us:

> Thus says the LORD: "Let not the wise man boast in his wisdom, let not the mighty man boast in his might, let not the rich man boast in his riches, but let him who boasts boast in this, that he understands and knows me, that I am the LORD who practices steadfast love, justice, and righteousness in the earth. For in these things I delight, declares the LORD."

Once while visiting Israel, Mally and I observed the ruins of temples built by Herod I at Caesarea-Philippi, Masada, and Jerusalem. In their prime, the buildings were magnificent. Herod invested his wealth and time to leave a legacy of great buildings . . . but he wasn't at all interested in the eternal state of his soul or others. What is the result of his priorities? Herod has been dead almost 2,000 years — and now there is hardly anything left of his palaces. They are basically just a pile of weathered stones. He lived in luxury on earth, but all these material things have basically disappeared — yet Herod's soul lives on in eternity! Jesus, in Mark 8:36–37, puts the issue in perspective with these words: "For what does it profit a man to gain the whole world, and forfeit his soul? For what can a man give in return for his soul?"

Mum and Dad were more interested in eternal matters rather than the materialism of this world. They committed their time and finances to leaving a legacy that would last forever — children who trusted Christ for salvation, who married Christian mates to produce godly offspring for the Lord. I could never thank them enough for the impact that their efforts had on me. It was an impact that was direct and eternal. Matthew 6:19–21 really sums up the difference between my parents and Herod I:

> Do not lay up for yourselves treasures on earth, where moth and rust destroy and where thieves break in and steal, but lay up for yourselves treasures in heaven, where neither moth nor rust destroys and where thieves do not break in and steal. For where your treasure is, there your heart will be also.

What kind of legacy are you building?

Are you striving for earthly position and riches that are meaningless compared to the importance of knowing the Lord? When you are dead and your children and their children look back at your life, what kind of priorities will they see? What will they say about you?

The Challenge Before Us

As a Christian parent, you would do well to look forward and think about your grandchildren or great-grandchildren, maybe even your great-great-grandchildren. Think about this: Do you see godly offspring, or do you see generations who have not been given a godly inheritance? Within the sovereignty of God, much will depend on you.

You may need to sustain a godly heritage left by your ancestors, or you may need to start from scratch and re-create a legacy that has been lost. Either way, this is the great challenge before us. My summary of what we should be doing as parents follows.

We are to raise godly seed by accepting our responsibilities as parents and to see our children conformed to the image of Christ, diligently training them in truth, using the rod with love, remembering God's warnings and blessings promised — so that our children will not learn the ways of the heathen, but will be able to distinguish good from evil, be equipped to stand against the giants that oppose Christianity, and so influence the world for Christ.

That is not only a great challenge, it is an important one. The way we train our children will affect the way they train their children and so on, generation after generation. The present generation does not need to be lost. A godly legacy can be maintained; a lost legacy can be reclaimed. By the strength of grace and His Spirit in us, with the truth of His Word to instruct us, we can raise godly children in this ungodly world. The process begins with you, and you must begin with a compelling conviction that leads you to prioritize training up a godly generation. That is the first essential component for building a godly legacy.

Let us then search the Scriptures and determine what the biblical standards for families are and then apply them so we can practically know how to train up godly seed. However, I want to warn you, as we uncover the biblical principles we are called to, you may be challenged and convicted like never before.

What lies ahead is real, down to earth, and very convicting. In my plain, straight Aussie English, the chapters ahead are very forthright and to the point, and I don't pull any punches — but then neither does Scripture when it speaks on this issue! So be prepared!

I hope you will read on with great anticipation and excitement. I trust what is written may help to change (if it is necessary) the direction your family is heading. Generations to come may be affected if you apply consistently the teachings of Scripture in this vital area.

Key thoughts from this chapter:

1. History clearly shows that an entire legacy can be lost in one generation.

2. The family is the first and most fundamental of all human institutions ordained in Scripture. It is vital as the backbone of a nation and to provide godly offspring for the next generation.

3. The consequences of an ungodly legacy are incalculable. The priority for training godly children is a multigenerational priority, and therefore, it is essential that we have a multi-generational view of what we leave.

4. The first "component for a godly legacy" is a compelling conviction that leads us to prioritize training up a godly generation.

CHAPTER FOUR

DILIGENT DADS

∾

This chapter will deal with the role of the father and the next chapter largely with the role of the mother. The perspective you will gain is very important, for the ideal situation in a family is two parents working toward the same goals in a way that complements each other's strengths and compensates for each other's weaknesses. If that is not the case, and you are doing this solo (which can be the case for many different reasons), you'll still appreciate a deeper understanding of the complete task that lies ahead. At the end of the next chapter, we will pull it all together and give you an opportunity to make a definitive commitment to leaving a godly legacy. And for those in a situation less than what God's plan for the family is, I believe God will give a special measure of grace to help you in this vital task.

Much confusion exists on the topic of parental roles — and where there appears to be clarity, so often it is wrapped in so much cliché that the practical applications become lost in meaningless rhetoric. So let's look to God's Word for clarity on this vital topic.

Let me start with an idea that is both simple and profound: God has a special plan for you. Please let that thought soak in. God has a special plan for you. That is something that people have been telling me my whole life. I believe it, and I'm telling you the same now. You are not here by accident or by chance. You are here as part of a greater plan — it's a plan God has prepared, and it's a plan that involves you.

My mum has told me that when I was just a babe, a snake nearly attacked me while I sat in a stroller. Mum grabbed me and pulled me to safety. As a child, I was very sick. Several times, my parents had to take me to the hospital for life-threatening emergencies that required driving through the rutted outback and forging flooded rivers to get me to help, but my mum always felt that I would be okay. She somehow knew that God had some sort of special plan for me. As a teen, my grandma (we called her Nana) also told me this, and sometimes when I would read the Bible out front in church, others would say the same. I've come to believe that God does have a special plan for me, just as He has one for you. In His marvelous Word, He has made that plan known, calling us to be diligent dads and mothers of faith.

Diligent Dads

Throughout the Scriptures, our special roles and responsibilities are revealed. Consider these piercing passages directed to fathers:

> The father makes known to the children your faithfulness (Isaiah 38:19).

> Fathers . . . bring them up in the discipline and instruction of the Lord (Ephesians 6:4).

> For I have chosen him, that he may command his children and his household after him to keep the way of the LORD by doing righteousness and justice, so that the LORD may bring to Abraham what he has promised him (Genesis 18:19).

These are just a few of the many verses that mention fathers in regard to training children. There is another passage of Scripture that I want you to read carefully. Note the words that are emphasized in bold:

> Give ear, O my people, to my teaching; incline your ears to the words of my mouth! I will open my mouth in a parable; I will utter dark sayings from of old, things that we have heard and known, that our **fathers** have told us. We will not hide them from their **children**, but tell to the coming generation the glorious deeds of the LORD, and his might, and the wonders that he has done. He established a testimony in Jacob and appointed a law in Israel, which he commanded our **fathers** to teach to their **children**, that the next generation might know them, the **children** yet unborn, and arise and tell them to their **children**, so that they should set their hope in God and not forget the works of God, but keep his commandments (Psalm 78:1–7; emphasis added).

Psalm 78 is a long one, but I encourage you to read it through, and even write it down and keep it as a bookmark as you are studying this book. The psalm is saying over and over: Fathers, teach your children so they'll not forget to teach their children, so that they might not forget what God has done and keep His commandments.

Sadly, in other parts of Psalm 78, we read that the Israelites did forget the works of God. They ended up adopting the pagan religions of the day and fell into sin because the fathers did not teach the children. One of mankind's biggest problems is forgetting what God has said or done. In the New Testament, Peter says over and over again, "I want to put you in remembrance of these things." Paul makes the same sort of statements. Why? Because God knows we are only too apt to forget.

A pastor once said to me, "My congregation has seen your videos, and some went to a creation seminar a couple of years ago. Do you think they need to come to the seminar you're running in the area?" I answered, "Pastor, how many of your congregation remember what you preached last Sunday?" The pastor replied, "They'll be at the seminar!"

If you have read the Old Testament, you are familiar with the accounts of the Israelites and how God did marvelous and miraculous things for them. Sadly, though, they kept forgetting what God had done for them, and then they would complain and end up in trouble. When I read these accounts to my children, they often used to say, "Dad, how come they were so stupid?! Why couldn't they remember how God took them through the Red Sea, or gave them manna from heaven, or warned them with fire from heaven? What was wrong with them, Dad?"

Well, they had the same problem we have. In fact, we are no different from the Israelites. We are only too apt to forget. How many times have we heard a great sermon at church and been convicted to apply a particular biblical principle in our lives, only to forget the principle after a few days or weeks? Then one day we hear a message on the same biblical principle, and we are reminded of something we should not have forgotten. The great Psalms of the Bible begin with this admonition:

> Blessed is the man who walks not in the counsel of the wicked, nor stands in the way of sinners, nor sits in the seat of scoffers; but his delight is in the law of the LORD, and on his law he meditates day and night (Psalm 1:1–2).

Remember how the Israelites crossed the Jordan River under the leadership of Joshua? A miracle performed by God. What did God tell them to do in Joshua 4:1–9? He told them to take 12 stones from what at that time of year was a fast-flowing river, from the bottom, and build a monument with the stones so that when their children asked, "What do these stones mean?" they would not forget to tell them what God had done.

Sadly, they do forget, and what happened with the Israelites stands as a warning for us. After Joshua and all the generation that lived with him died, the Bible records these words from Judges 2:10–13:

> And all that generation also were gathered to their fathers. And there arose another generation after them who did not know the LORD or the work that he had done for Israel. And the people of Israel did what was evil in the sight of the LORD and served the Baals. And they abandoned the LORD, the God of their fathers, who had brought them out of the

> land of Egypt. They went after other gods, from among the gods of the peoples who were around them and bowed down to them. And they provoked the LORD to anger. They abandoned the LORD and served the Baals and the Ashtaroth.

The Israelites lost it — and in only one generation. How? Psalm 78 relates the sad event. The fathers forgot the great works God did for them, and they obviously didn't teach the children like they should have. Did the fathers have excuses? I'm sure they did, just like Christian fathers today who shrug off their responsibility with excuses like these: "The kids are going to church; they attend youth group; they go to a Christian school — they'll be okay." I believe the Israelite fathers assumed because they knew about the great things God had done, that their children would somehow know about these things. Such acts were basically taken for granted by the fathers, so they did not "remember" them by acknowledging them and communicating them to subsequent generations.

However, because we are born sinners, the truth needs to be taught carefully to each generation — our fallen human nature is such that we don't want truth before God saves us, and we continually struggle with the desire to sin after. Romans 3:10–11 says that "as it is written: 'None is righteous, no, not one; no one understands; no one seeks for God.' "

Therefore, it is absolutely vital that we continually remind our children and ourselves of the truth.

Role Reversal

Let me ask you another question I have asked of thousands upon thousands of people at seminars and meetings in different parts of the world: In the majority of Christian homes in our Western nations, is it the father or the mother who trains the children spiritually? Who really is the spiritual head of the house? Who is taking the responsibility for teaching scriptural truths to the children? Who teaches them to pray and how to act as a Christian? Is it usually the mom or dad?

You know the answer I have been given on every occasion I have asked this question, don't you? I'm sure you would give me the same answer! In the majority of Christian homes, it is usually the mother, not the father, who acts as the spiritual head. (In too many cases, neither the mother nor the father is fulfilling the responsibility to train their children in the things of God.) In the homes where some training is happening, the mother is usually the one that teaches, prays, and reads the Scriptures without her husband's help. *It's a reversal of God-given roles, and it's not right.*

Mothers seem to be taking on the leadership roles more and more, and fathers are opting out of this area all together.

This is one of the greatest problems that exists in Christian homes today. In the majority of Christian homes, it is not the father who is the spiritual head of, or the priest to, his family. Most fathers have neglected their biblical role as the spiritual head. They have abandoned their responsibility.

Another consequence of this problem I have observed (and heard the same from parents as I have traveled extensively) is that there's a sore lack of spiritual young men in our churches. This then is a contributing factor to the lack of godly offspring in the coming generations.

Delinquent Dads

One of the greatest travesties in our society today is that many fathers are not transmitting to the next generation the knowledge of God and His commands from the Word. What is even sadder is that most fathers don't seem to know how to do this. They don't know what it means to be the spiritual head of the house. It appears that many of the fathers of the past did not transmit this knowledge to the present generation and now we have a generation of fathers that has very little, if any, understanding of what the family is all about, and so few have trained them or modeled to them spiritual leadership or how to be a Christian father.

Because the legacy has been broken, men in general don't know why they should lead (they are missing that compelling conviction and the significance of their God-given roles), and they don't know how to lead. I have had fathers come up to me and tell me that their father did not read to them or teach them or pray with them. They almost feel "sissy" doing this with their children because the strongest males in their lives didn't model any of it. Their image of masculinity is missing the spiritual component. Many Christian dads have been given no tools, no blueprint, and no materials with which to build their legacy . . . and because many know they should be leading, they are left with heavy guilt and feelings of inadequacy.

In many homes, the fathers won't (or think they can't) be the spiritual head and deliberately leave it to their wives. I do praise the Lord for the wives who take on the task to ensure their children obtain biblical training. Some wives have told me they have pleaded with their husbands to head up the spiritual training in their homes — but many times to no avail. But then there's also a problem that some wives want to be the head of the family. That's another issue we will take up in the next chapter.

This is in direct disobedience to what God has clearly commanded. Dad, are you the spiritual head of your family? If not, let me warn you about something here. There are serious consequences that arise out of this neglect, and one of the most grave is homosexuality. I have a good friend in Australia who ministers to men caught up in the homosexual movement. He, and others who are involved in this counseling, tell me that there is a very definite correlation between a domineering mother in the home, together with a lack of male leadership, and boys turning to homosexual behavior.[1] (This doesn't mean that those who choose to sin in this way are not personally responsible for the decision to do so, but it does show how our parenting can contribute to the choices they make.) If we don't

1. https://fathersforlife.org/dale/childhood_of_homosexual_men_ToC.htm.

do things God's way, there will always be negative consequences.

As a teacher, I taught my students that the only basis for marriage was in the Bible, back in Genesis. I taught them that sex outside of marriage was against God's rules. I explained to them that marriage made them one with their spouse, just as Adam and Eve were one flesh. I showed them that God, as their Creator, had complete rights over their lives, and that if they wanted their marriage to work, they needed to obey the rules for marriage — the rules set up by the One who created marriage in the first place. Of course, for Christians, I showed them from Scripture they could never even consider looking at a man or woman as a prospective husband or wife if that person was not also a Christian. I'm glad that I got to share this with my students, but quite frankly, it wasn't my job or responsibility. Teaching the children is the job of the dad. I believe that the more fathers obey the Scripture in this area, the more Christian families can be on fire for the Lord as they were created to be.

The challenge for every father is to pass on the spiritual inheritance you received from your family (if you were blessed enough to receive one) or to re-create a lost legacy if the fathers before you neglected to do so. Remember, regardless of the past, the future is your responsibility. You might have some good excuses, but the excuses end here. God says it's your job no matter what.

Remember Psalm 78? Dads, you are to be diligent to impart the knowledge of God to the next generation, period. You can easily learn to do this. We will show you how to get started shortly, but you must be committed. If you are more interested in your business or football or television, if you are giving your best to your career and come home at night too tired to even bother spending time with your children (let alone pray and read the Word with them), then you are making a big mistake. Who is really training your kids? The TV? The kids across the street? The internet? Video games and movies? Dad, don't stick your head in the sand on this one. You've only got one shot at this. Don't let the opportunity to train your children pass you by . . . the stakes are just too high for everyone.

At one church I was speaking at, a man came up to me with tears in his eyes and said, "Please, I have three children, I want to train them properly, but I don't know how. No one has ever trained me to be a father. Please can you help me?" This man (and many others) is one of the reasons I believe that the

Lord has burdened me to write this book. I want to help fathers to know what God thinks about training children. The great scientist Johannes Kepler allegedly said something like, "I want to think God's thoughts after Him." When it comes to building a godly legacy, we are wise to want to think God's thoughts as well.

You can read all sorts of books and take all sorts of classes on parenting and being a spiritual leader, but when it all comes down to it, the very most important thing you can do is just do it.

You are never going to do it perfectly, so you might as well just jump in and start. Here are some simple things that you can do right now that will help begin making a huge difference in your family:

1. Pray with your wife. This may seem awkward at the start, but again, just do it. Pray before meals. Pray in bed at night. Pray together for each of your kids as they sleep.

2. Pray for and with your kids. Bedtime is an ideal place to get started. When you get them tucked in, just take them by the hand and let them listen as you thank God for them and ask for His blessings on their lives. (They love that!) Ask them if they have any requests

that you can pray for. In time, ask them if they want to pray out loud with you, but let them know that God always hears their silent prayers, too.

3. Study the Bible. Start reading your Bible where your family can see you. (You don't want to do this for show like the Pharisees; you do it as an authentic model for your family.) Then start reading it to them. A good place to start is Genesis 1–11 — the foundation of the rest of the Bible. Also study the Psalms or Proverbs. If it's December, start with what we call "the Christmas Message" — the babe in a manger. If it's spring (in the Northern Hemisphere), read the passages pertaining to Easter — the death and Resurrection of our Savior. Start in Revelation. Start anywhere you want — but do it in a planned way — using a particular book of the Bible, verses pertaining to a particular subject, etc. In time, let them read it to you . . . you're training them to continue the legacy with their future family, remember? You will have a lifetime to get better at it, but most importantly, just start NOW!

4. Teach them apologetics and to learn how to think foundationally. I will explain this in

another chapter. Obtain Answers in Genesis[2] resources to help you with this.

5. Go to a good church and get plugged in. You might have to search for a while to find one that really ministers and teaches according to the Word of God. You might have to leave the church where you've been a member for decades, but find one that upholds the content and the authority of the Bible, and just start going there. (Remember, if you're looking for the "perfect" church, don't join it because you'll spoil it! There is no "perfect church," but it is so important for the family to be a part of a local church — one that really upholds the truth of Scripture.)

Have fun and, yes, you will make lots of mistakes — but just do it. Because when you are long dead, will your children and children's children remember you as the spiritual head of your house who poured out sacrificial love? Will they remember that the Bible was the axiom and foundation of your home? Will they remember you for your stand on biblical authority and your love for them as you trained them to be godly offspring in this fallen world?

---

2. Answersingenesis.org.

Be a diligent dad. Do it for the sake of your kids and future generations. It's your role, and it's the right thing to do.

Key thoughts from this chapter:

1. The Bible tells us that we are, and have, forgetful children. The father of the home must constantly remind his household of God's goodness and truth.

2. Spiritual headship is the responsibility of the father. Too many fathers have become delinquent dads who are not fulfilling their God-given role.

3. Now is the time to begin. Pray with your wife and children, read the Bible together, and get involved in a good church. Take the initiative now; later is too late.

4. Forget being perfect and just do it! When you fall short or forget, just get up and do it again. In the long run, your efforts will make a huge difference.

A GIRL

NAMED RUTH

On October 22, 1971, while sitting in a car looking over the sea at a place called "Manly" in Brisbane, Australia, I asked Mally to marry me. (Can you imagine getting engaged at "Manly"?!) At the moment she said those beautiful words "I will!" neither of us had any idea of where the Lord would lead us. Many years later, I realized how God had been preparing each of us for the special ministry we were to be called into, for 15 years later, in 1986, Mally and I made an important decision that would change our lives dramatically.

After visiting the United States on speaking tours in the early eighties, I realized that most of the churches in America did not understand the importance of the Book of Genesis and that many had compromised with the issues of evolution and the age of the earth. I also recognized that America was the greatest Christianized nation on earth and the center of the economic world. The Lord had burdened us with the desire to see the relevance of the creation message proclaimed around the world. It was obvious that, if the creation apologetics ministry we had begun in Australia was to have a worldwide impact, we had to be active in the United States. After much prayer and seeking counsel and wisdom from others, we were convinced we had to leave Australia and begin ministry in the United States full-time.

The decision was not easy. It meant leaving our family roots and saying goodbye to our homeland. It meant we would face many cultural differences and much spiritual opposition. We knew that the move would be particularly demanding and costly for Mally. Gone would be her support structure and the stability of life in familiar circumstances. Mally is considerably shy, but as we faced the decision, her strength, commitment, and devotion showed strong. She was first and foremost committed to God, willing to make great sacrifices for His kingdom. Secondly, she showed remarkable willingness to support me in the ministry I believed God was calling me to. God matched her faithfulness with His provision and a special confirmation that we were on the right track.

Toward the end of that year, we attended the wedding of one of our friends. The pastor was the father of the groom. As part of his address during the ceremony, he turned to his soon-to-be daughter-in-law and read from Ruth 1:8–18:

> But Naomi said to her two daughters-in-law, "Go, return each of you to her mother's house. May the LORD deal kindly with you, as you have dealt with the dead and with me. The LORD grant that you may find rest, each of you in the house of her husband!" Then she kissed them, and they lifted up their voices and wept. And they said to her, "No, we will return with you to your people." But Naomi said, "Turn back, my daughters; why will you go with me? Have I yet sons in my womb that they may become your husbands? Turn back, my daughters; go your way, for I am too old to have a husband. If I should say I have hope, even if I should have a husband this night and should bear sons, would you therefore wait till they were grown? Would you therefore refrain from marrying? No, my daughters,

> for it is exceedingly bitter to me for your sake that the hand of the LORD has gone out against me." Then they lifted up their voices and wept again. And Orpah kissed her mother-in-law, but Ruth clung to her.
>
> And she said, "See, your sister-in-law has gone back to her people and to her gods; return after your sister-in-law." But Ruth said, "Do not urge me to leave you or to return from following you. *For where you go I will go, and where you lodge I will lodge. Your people shall be my people, and your God my God. Where you die I will die, and there will I be buried.* May the LORD do so to me and more also if anything but death parts me from you." And when Naomi saw that she was determined to go with her, she said no more [emphasis added].

At the time, we were making the decision whether to move to the United States or not. We were also in the process of being admitted into membership in a new church. The church we had attended moved farther out into the suburbs, so a number of members were being transferred to a different church of the same denomination.

At this new church, the pastor had a particular way of admitting new members. He would call the people out to the front and then interview them and ask them to give a short testimony about why they were joining the church.

Now Mally is a very quiet, shy person. She is not a public speaker and has no desire to be one. In fact, she is sometimes intimidated by just meeting people — she would be terrified if she had to speak to a group of people. We had been talking about this and what would happen when we were to be admitted into membership at this new church. During the wedding, when the pastor was reading from Ruth, Mally turned to me and said, "You know, I'm like Ruth. Where you go, I go. Your God is my God. I support you totally because that is what God has called me to do. We are in this together. How about I just say that at the church when the pastor asks for my testimony?"

A couple of weeks later, we were at our new church and the pastor called all the people being admitted into membership to come forward. Because of the unique situation of people being transferred from the other church, there were a large number of people standing at the front.

As the pastor approached people, instead of asking them for a testimony (as was his normal way of doing things), he decided he would say something about each person. He was aware of the decision Mally and I were considering to move to the United States, but he knew nothing about what Mally had decided to say, and he really didn't know about the emotional struggle we were going through in regard to this decision.

When he came to Mally, he looked at her and said, "Mally, I've watched you and have known Ken's family for many years. I see how supportive you are of Ken's ministry. In thinking about you, it came to me that you reminded me of Ruth. Where Ken goes, you go. His God is your God. You support him totally in the ministry God has called him into."

Wow. To us this was a special seal from the Lord that we were making the right decision. There was such a peace in our hearts as we began the process of packing up to move to a different country. Yes, the Lord had called us to share our "inheritance" with more of the world.

The Role of a Godly Mom

Just as God made the role of a diligent dad clear, He has also made His intentions known regarding the role of a godly wife. Like so many other essential doctrines, the role of the woman is first established in Genesis:

> The LORD God took the man and put him in the garden of Eden to work it and keep it. . . . Then the LORD God said, "It is not good that the man should be alone; I will make him a helper fit for him." . . . So the LORD God caused a deep sleep to fall upon the man, and while he slept took one of his ribs and closed up its place with flesh. And the rib that the LORD God had taken from the man he made into a woman and brought her to the man. . . . Therefore a man shall leave his father and his mother and hold fast to his wife, and they shall become one flesh. And the man and his wife were both naked and were not ashamed (Genesis 2:15–25).

In the midst of our fallen world, it is important to remember that this was God's good and original design. We would do well to reclaim as much of it in Christ as we can. God fashioned a woman to complete what was lacking in Adam, that she might become his helper, that the two of them would truly become one.

Many other passages from God's Word reveal the role that God has designed for wives and mothers. One of the more pointed and all-encompassing is found in Proverbs 31:10–31. (This was one of my father's favorite Scripture passages. I used to hear him quote it often in relation to his thankfulness for the gift of his wife, my mother.) The verses paint a beautiful picture of the woman God designed mothers to be. Here are some excerpts:

> An excellent wife, who can find? She is far more precious than jewels. The heart of her husband trusts in her. . . . She does him good and not harm. . . . She rises while it is yet night and provides food for her household. . . . She considers a field and buys it; with the fruit of her hands she plants a vineyard. . . . She opens her hand to the poor. . . . Strength and dignity are her clothing. . . . She opens her mouth with wisdom.

These passages reveal many virtues of a woman committed to building a godly legacy for her family.

She is encouraged to be a woman of character, integrity, and action. The passages even endorse her role as a respected businesswoman in the marketplace. Certainly, mothers should also be involved in teaching their children spiritual truths.

I praise the Lord for my godly mother who prayed with us when we were small and continued to pray daily for us until she received her eternal reward in heaven in November 2019. She stood as my father did on the authority of God's Word and would witness to whomever she came in contact with if given the opportunity. There was no doubt that Dad was the spiritual head and that our mother supported him in this role 100 percent. Whether it was cooking for visitors, supporting school functions, waiting up for Dad to return from school and church meetings, organizing missionary visits — I never had any inkling that they didn't do everything together as one. Mum also balanced out Dad in various ways. Her strengths made up for his weaknesses and vice versa.

Fathers are to be the overall spiritual head. Whenever and wherever possible, the father's leadership should be as obvious to the children as it is to the wife. The task of raising godly children in an ungodly world takes teamwork. My wife and I do this together when I am home, and Mally covers for me when I'm on the road ministering. Overall, our children know and observe that I take on the headship role and Mally takes on the helpmate role. We both submit to each other in the roles God has for each of us: "submitting to one another out of reverence for Christ" (Ephesians 5:21).

That is the way we were created to function, but in the modern world we often see the opposite, where the mother is leading and the dad is following. This is even reinforced by most Christian children's books I have seen where mention of spiritual leadership is made. Many of these books will picture a mother with the Bible open, reading it to her children, or they will instruct the children to tell their mother something or ask for her advice. Look closely at the books you have for your children and I am sure you will see that this is a characteristic of many children's materials available for the Christian market today.

On top of this, more women are becoming increasingly domineering as they take over the position as head of the home. The more I travel and meet families around the world, the more obvious it appears to me that the feminist movement has affected many women in our churches — and this affects the whole family structure.

Actually, God's Word warns us about what will happen to husbands and wives as a result of our sin nature. In Genesis 3:16 we read, "To the woman he said, 'I will surely multiply your pain in childbearing;

in pain you shall bring forth children. Your desire shall be contrary to your husband, but he shall rule over you.'" Now when we consider this passage, we should probably see the same meaning in regard to Cain in Genesis 4:7 and the desire of sin to rule over him — sin is crouching at the door in the sinful desire of woman. So when Genesis 3:16 says, "Your desire shall be for your husband," it means that when sin has the upper hand in woman, she will desire to overpower or subdue or exploit or rule over man. And when sin has the upper hand in man, he will respond in like manner and with his strength subdue her, or rule over woman. What a warning for a woman not to usurp the man's role, and what a warning for man not to use his role to lord it despotically over women. Each of us needs to examine our own hearts in regard to this matter.

We are growing up in a world that emphasizes everyone has a right to their own opinions. We are indoctrinated through the public education system and the media that we have our rights. I remember one of the female teachers at a school I taught at in Australia telling the girls in her class, "Remember, if you get married, or just live with a guy, you have your rights — you are an individual." This contradicts God's design for a husband and wife to be "one," and this mindset can create serious confusion in the home.

Over the years I have observed a number of men in the Christian ministry who have had to give up the ministry, or greatly limit what they set out to do, because of an unsupportive spouse. I have also observed that some children of pastors and other full-time Christian workers rebel against Christianity. I know there are many and varied reasons for such situations. However, from my own observations and experience in traveling around the world, I do believe that one of the major factors relates very much to the fact that their wives could not cope with the husband being away or spending so much time in the demands of Christian work.

I've heard such wives question their husband's ministry in front of the children and others. The husband and wife were certainly not "one" in this regard. The wife's discontent was very obvious to the children. Now it's also true that some men in Christian work have greatly neglected their wives and children, forsaking their priority to be diligent dads, and that is also a problem. It's important for a mom to ask, "Am I fulfilling my role as a helpmate to my husband, or am I undermining his role as the spiritual head of our home?" And it's important for a dad to ask, "Am I fulfilling my role as a husband and father and loving my wife as I should?" Here is an important verse for husbands to meditate on: "Husbands, love your wives, as Christ loved the church and gave himself up for her" (Ephesians 5:25). Husbands, do you pour out that sort of sacrificial love on your wife?

The old saying is true: "Behind every good man is a good woman." The Ham children are blessed in heritage to be able to say that of our mother. While so many women are burdened with a heart for the superficial and material things of life, God has given a much greater responsibility, that of supportive substance — the type of supportive substance that is also founded and grounded in His mighty Word and shines like a beacon as an example to up and coming wives everywhere. In our case, God has provided not only a good wife and mother, but a good woman who is a mentor for women. Truly, my mother fulfilled this Scripture:

> Older women likewise are to be reverent in behavior, not slanderers or slaves to much wine. They are to teach what is good, and so train the young women to love their husbands and children, to be self-controlled, pure, working at home, kind, and submissive to their own

husbands, that the word of God may not be reviled (Titus 2:3–5).

There's another thing my mother was famous for — her cooking! Roast lamb, corned beef, Yorkshire pudding, exotic Aussie desserts, and much more — our mum was a chef extraordinaire! Usually when I went back to Australia to visit Mum, she had my favorite cakes (like lamingtons — YUM!) waiting for me. I know that there are other virtues that are more significant than cooking, but the atmosphere she created around the dinner table was a significant element in our family legacy, and my stomach is grateful!

The Biblical Ideal for Husbands and Wives

Consider the following from Ephesians 5:22–28:

Wives, submit to your own husbands, as to the Lord. For the husband is the head of the wife even as Christ is the head of the church, his body, and is himself its Savior. Now as the church submits to Christ, so also wives should submit in everything to their husbands.

Husbands, love your wives, as Christ loved the church and gave himself up for her, that he might sanctify her, having cleansed her by the washing of water with the word, so that he might present the church to himself in splendor, without spot or wrinkle or any such thing, that she might be holy and without blemish. In the same way husbands should love their wives as their own bodies. He who loves his wife loves himself.

Also, carefully consider Christ's example and how Peter relates that to the roles of husbands and wives in 1 Peter 2:21–3:7:

For to this you have been called, because Christ also suffered for you, leaving you an example, so that you might follow in his steps. He committed no sin, neither was deceit found in his mouth. When he was reviled, he did not revile in return; when he suffered, he did not threaten, but continued entrusting himself to him who judges justly. He himself bore our sins in his body on the tree, that we might die to sin and live to righteousness. By his wounds you have been healed. For you were straying like sheep, but have now returned to the Shepherd and Overseer of your souls. *Likewise, wives, be subject to your own husbands*, so that even if some do not obey the word, they may be won without a word by the conduct of their wives, when they see your respectful and pure conduct. Do not let your adorning be external — the braiding of hair and the putting on of gold jewelry, or the clothing you wear — but let your adorning be the hidden person of the heart with the imperishable beauty of a gentle and quiet spirit, which in God's sight is very precious. For this is how the holy women who hoped in God used to adorn themselves, by submitting to their own husbands, as Sarah obeyed Abraham, calling him lord. And you are her children, if you do good and do not fear anything that is frightening. *Likewise, husbands, live with your wives in an understanding way*, showing honor to the woman as the weaker vessel, since they are heirs with you of the grace of life, so that your prayers may not be hindered [emphasis added].

Both husband and wife are called to model their lives after Christ, and He was submissive to the point of death on the Cross.

That is some submission! Women should "in the same way" be submissive to their husbands. Husbands are to "in the same way" love their wives. That is some sacrificial love a husband is to pour out on his wife! As it states in Ephesians 5:25, "Husbands, love your wives, as Christ loved the church and gave himself up for her." Maybe if husbands loved their wives like this (with a sacrificial love), their wives wouldn't have a problem with godly submission. Maybe if wives were submissive to their husbands (with a sacrificial submission), they wouldn't have problems with husbands loving them as they should.

Dad and Mum may have had disagreements at times, as all couples no doubt do, but I cannot remember them having any fights in front of us. I remember them as a couple devoted to each other. They clearly showed they loved us, and they did what they should to train us up as godly offspring. What an example they were to us! I believe that such stability and obvious outworking of obedience to the Scripture by our parents had a major impact on all of us children — all who today have stable marriages where husbands and wives are totally devoted to each other. I could not even imagine what it must be like to have been brought up in a home without such stability, love, and devotion — and I can't help but wonder what sorts of issues marriage problems cause in the next generation.

The point is this: Both husbands and wives need to be obedient to what God says, and not to their opinions or feelings! That is God's ideal design for the family, but we do live in a less than perfect world because of sin and the curse. We have families that have mothers and fathers that cannot (or will not) fulfill their God-given roles. We have orphans. We have foster kids. We have widows and widowers. We have abusive homes. Single parents and those dealing with broken marriages have a very complicated and difficult task before them . . . and as I've stated before, I believe God gives a special measure of grace to men and women in these sad situations. Those of us who are aware of such families need to do whatever we can to support them and maybe even be role models for their children. These are the times when the Body is to work as a body, healing, supporting, and compensating for other parts of the body that are in need.

When Mally and I were making our decision to come to the United States, it was very difficult to consider leaving family and friends. We agonized over the decision day after day. Luke 14:26–27 says, "If anyone comes to me and does not hate his own father and mother and wife and children and brothers and sisters, yes, and even his own life, he cannot be my disciple. Whoever does not bear his own cross and come after me cannot be my disciple." We knew what we needed to do, but we also knew that it would leave a big hole in our extended family, particularly with me being on the road so much.

When we moved to San Diego in January of 1987, it was hard to make friends and learn how to live in a country that had many cultural differences, but God knew what we needed. The house we purchased "just happened" to be next door to a wonderful older couple who became "Grandma Jo" and "Poppa Bill" to our children. What a blessing! God was looking after us in special ways. Poppa Bill and Grandma Jo have left this earth now, but they were an excellent example of how God provided for our family.

Let's be honest. We live in a fallen world, and the perfect family doesn't exist. There are many families out there that need us to help them be whole and healthy. It's much easier to condemn and judge others for the circumstances they are in (often by their own making), but isn't this an opportunity for us, as members of Christ's body, to minister to others in His name? Isn't this an opportunity for us to be vulnerable and admit that we too need the help of others around us?

Poppa Bill and Grandma Jo filled a big spot in our hearts, but the move was still very difficult on Mally. She never complained, but I knew she was still lonely and greatly missed family. We prayed about this, and the Lord answered in a way we didn't expect. He gave us a baby daughter! Our California girl. What a special gift this was for all of us, particularly Mally.

As we thought about this answer to prayer and why we were in the United States, we decided to name our daughter Kristel Ruth Ham. She is a reminder to us of the seal that the Lord put on our ministry in the United States — and more than that, her name is a continual reminder to me that Mally is like Ruth — a supportive, devoted wife whom I love more now than I ever have.

Mally has said to me many times that she sees her role is to support me in whatever way she can so that I can carry out the ministry God has called me to be actively involved in. This has often been demanding and taxing on her, requiring that she fill in for me when I'm gone. (I don't know why, but it always seems that the washing machine waited to leak or the heater decided to blow when I'm away.) Usually, Mally never mentioned these things to me at the time, as she didn't want problems at home to detract from the ministry I'm involved in.

Her attitude was obvious to our children. There is no doubt in their minds at all that their mother supports their dad 100 percent. I believe this has had a lot to do with why our children have not rebelled against my absences and the reason why they are so supportive (just like their mother) of the itinerant creation apologetics ministry I am actively a part of. Now they are bringing up our grandchildren to love the Answers in Genesis ministry and the Creation Museum and Ark Encounter attractions.

I could write an entire book about how Mally has been the best helpmate I could ever have. I love her more every day and could not even express in words how much I appreciate her and love her as a wife. She is also a wonderful mother and grandmother (Nannan to our 17 [currently] grandkids) — always putting others first and herself last. When it comes to Answers in Genesis, Mally has made all the difference in the world — and I mean that literally: The world is different because of her. I seem to get so much of the credit from people, but let there be no doubt that God uses Mally and the gifts and strength he has given her in amazing ways. He has used her sacrifice and support (as well as her willingness to put up with my faults and cover for my weaknesses!) to make this ministry what it is. There's no way the Answers in Genesis ministry and the two attractions would be as they are today without her. Only God knows the personal sacrifice she has given for our family and for the ministry.

I'm truly blessed by the Lord every time I see committed, godly parents — those who are living according to the roles given us in the Bible. Mally also rejoices in parents who are totally committed to the truth of Scripture and display this to their children. When parents choose to obey God and fulfill their God-given roles as described in Scripture, God's grace and blessings abound to all around and He is glorified.

As I look back at the legacy left by my father, there is no doubt that Mum's presence was a definitive factor in the inheritance he was able to leave. The godly leadership of my father was evident in the way my mother loved and supported him in return, as well as in the way she endlessly cared for us children. After Dad's passing, she also had her fair share of health issues, including cancer. I have witnessed my brothers and sisters rally together in assisting Mum in so many different ways. I interpret this as the gratitude we all have for the biblical heritage Mum and Dad have striven so hard over the years to supply. In fact, we see it as a true privilege and service not only to our mother, but our Sovereign Lord.

These words would undoubtedly make Mum uncomfortable. She would be the first to point out that any good in her came not from herself, but from the work of God in her and through her. Like the rest of us, she was made of sinful flesh, but she had also chosen to submit to the Word of God and the Holy Spirit. His truth and His presence in her accomplished holy things. She has been a supportive substance, a gentle but strong balancing presence, a defender of truth, a godly trainer of her children, and a powerful mentor of women in the Lord. When she passed away, a number of women from the nursing home she spent nearly two years in came to the memorial service to honor a woman who had so impacted them spiritually.

Mum would also have had difficulty with these words because she has never been one to seek out or expect recognition or praise. But it is only fitting. At the end of the description of an excellent wife in Proverbs 31, it says:

> Her children rise up and call her blessed; her husband also, and he praises her: "Many women have done excellently, but you surpass them all." Charm is deceitful, and beauty is vain, but a woman who fears the LORD is to be praised (Proverbs 31:28–30).

Yes, I call my mother blessed. And yes, our children and I call Mally blessed. Let God's Word be proven true again!

Pulling It All Together

There are three essential components for building a godly legacy: (1) a compelling conviction that leads us to prioritize training up a godly generation, (2) your personal relationship with God through Jesus Christ, and (3) a clear understanding of your roles and responsibilities.

Each of these components is necessary. If you try to build the legacy without even one of them, it will not last. None of these components will lead to a godly inheritance for your children unless you actually commit to acting on them . . . and that can be difficult to do if you feel like you must implement these components on your own. Thankfully, that is not the case. Consider these two passages:

> Abide in me, and I in you. As the branch cannot bear fruit by itself, unless it abides in the vine, neither can you, unless you abide in me. I am the vine; you are the branches. Whoever abides in me and I in him, he it is that bears much fruit, for apart from me you can do nothing (John 15:4–5).
>
> I can do all things through him who strengthens me (Philippians 4:13).

The three components are essential, and the commitment must be yours, but your real challenge is to be dependent on Him to fulfill the very things He commands you to do. Understanding this will give you strength when times are tough and ensure that He gets the glory for all the blessings.

If you and your spouse are "one" in the matters I have written about in the preceding chapters, I would invite you to come together and make the following prayer of commitment as husband and wife. If you are a single parent or you must build a legacy without the support of your mate, I invite you to make this commitment as well, knowing that God Himself will be your partner as you endeavor to raise godly children in this ungodly world.

Our God and our Creator,

We come to You now with empty hands, recognizing that all we are and all we have is a gift from You. You have made all things, and nothing has come into being that You have not made. We praise You for the children You have entrusted to us, and we deeply desire to build a godly legacy that will be a blessed inheritance to them, to their children, and to the generations to follow.

It is clear that Your Word, and only Your Word, can be the foundation for this legacy. The empty opinions of man and the fallible wisdom of the world can never be a substitute for Your perfect and living Word. Give us the willingness to search the Scriptures to discover the principles and commands that You have given us to obey.

Father, we humbly fear that the knowledge of You can be lost in a single generation. By the truth of our Word, and by the power of Your Spirit, we ask that You instill in our hearts a compelling conviction that leads us to prioritize the task of training up a godly generation.

Increase our love for You in our personal relationship with You through Jesus Christ so that we might be an authentic model to our children and that we might be empowered in our tasks by the very presence of You in our hearts. Give us a clear understanding of the roles and responsibilities You have created us to fulfill.

Our sinful tendencies will try to lead us into disobedience to Your will. We know that without You, we can do nothing, but that through Jesus Christ, we can do all things. Lord, we place ourselves humbly in Your hands. Use us as You see fit to be sacrificial, submissive, and loving to each other and to our children, that we might be used to build a godly legacy and leave a rich spiritual inheritance that brings glory, honor, and dominion to You and You only.

Amen

Key thoughts from this chapter:

1. Wives and mothers have an important role of support in the home. This role is described in Genesis 2, Proverbs 31, and many other places in Scripture.

2. In our fallen world, role reversal is common and unfortunate. Believers should seek to minister to those who are living in less than ideal circumstances.

3. Submission and sacrifice is the model given to wives by Christ. Love and sacrifice is the model Christ gives to the husband.

4. Supporting the strong Christian leadership of a godly father is the strongest adhesive a wife brings in building a biblical legacy.

CHAPTER SIX

POLAROID

BABIES

There is a time for everything,
and a season for every activity under the
heavens:
a time to be born and a time to die,
a time to plant and a time to uproot
(Ecclesiastes 3:1–2; NIV).

Let's be honest: It's a lot easier to make babies than it is to raise them — at least from a male's perspective! Mally and I had five beautiful children. We called them "Polaroid Babies" because it seemed Mally could deliver children at the press of a button. Remember when polaroid cameras were invented (and now they're coming back into popularity with the younger generations), and with the push of a button, the camera would take a photograph and push out a developed photo almost instantaneously. Well, you find out below why I call our children "polaroid babies."

Our firstborn came into the world on November 10, 1976, in the rural town of Dalby, Queensland, in Australia. Mally had been in labor almost seven hours, but a lot of this was because of the size of Nathan's head. The doctor warned us that the baby had a large hematoma. Nobody was quite sure what that was, but it made our son look like he had two heads for a while. Oh well, like they always say, "Two heads are better than one." His baby pictures were cute, though, and Nathan has grown into a fine man.

On February 22, 1978, Mally went into labor with our second child . . . and #2 sure knew how to make a grand entrance. Mally sensed right away that we needed to get to the hospital now. I tried counting contractions (you know, like a good husband is supposed to), but I couldn't count fast enough and called the ambulance in a somewhat panicked state . . . and of course the person who answered tried to be calm, asking, "Mr. Ham, is this your first or second? How far apart are the contractions?" I blurted out something to the effect that what was happening wasn't normal and they needed to get there immediately. I was told, "Yes, Mr. Ham, we'll send someone. Just stay calm." They didn't believe me, so I took the issue to the top and called on Mum! She called a friend who was a midwife.

When Mum took one look at the situation, she knew the baby was well on the way. She had six of her own but had never been on the receiving end of a delivery. She ran for the kitchen to make preparations. I was stressed out of my mind, praying like I had never prayed before, hoping the ambulance would show up. That's when Mally called for me. I raced to her side to see the baby's head appearing. I grabbed the baby as it delivered. Relying on my vast medical experience gained from the movies, I held the baby by the feet and spanked it — and the baby started to cry, just like it was supposed to (just like I saw in the movies). Then I remembered seeing doctors clean out the baby's mouth, so I put my finger in its mouth and kind of moved it around, hoping it cleared whatever it was supposed to.

Mum's midwife friend arrived. She asked for something to tie the cord with. Again, probably from a movie, I remembered hearing that people have used their boot laces to cut the umbilical cord, so I pulled out my boot lace and then stood there, without a clue of what to do next. Mum's friend was trained as a midwife and calmly took over. She took the bootlace and tied the cord and prepared Mally for the ambulance. As the paramedics walked up the stairs, I handed them a baby, mumbling something about the fact that they should have believed me and arrived earlier!

At the hospital, one of the nurses asked me, "So, is it a boy or girl?" I embarrassingly replied, "I don't know, I forgot to look!" But Mally calmly told me she knew as soon as she was born! We named her Renee Elizabeth. Mally was in labor for only 45 minutes, and we'll never know for sure if this had some sort of lasting effect on Renee — but she became a nurse and learned how to deliver babies! Then she worked as my executive assistant at Answers in Genesis for many years before founding our Christian school, Twelve Stones Christian Academy. Now she delivers lots of kids to their parents each day after watching over their Christian worldview educational training.

We were so sure that #3 would be a boy (well, Mally told me so) that we had the name Daniel chosen ahead of time. Although, if a girl, Mally said she liked Danielle. Well, she saw the light of day

September 14, 1982, after only 40 minutes of labor . . . and a nurse said, "Well, you will need to call her Danielle." Her full name is Danielle Marylyn. Many people probably don't know that Mally is actually a nickname given to her as a child by her mother — her real name is Marylyn.

Child #4 came in 1984. On September 29, Mally told me that it was time. I called the ambulance company, who (now well aware of the history of the Ham family) made it to the door in about 17.3 seconds. Still, Jeremy was born halfway to the hospital, only 11 minutes after the first contraction. He delivered in the back of an ambulance early in the evening, under a tree overlooking the city of Brisbane. I told Mally, "At least you had a nice romantic view of the city while he was being delivered!" (She didn't seem to appreciate that comment for some reason.) The tree is actually very near the center of Brisbane city. It's a Jackson fig tree. Whenever we visit Australia and go to the city of Brisbane, we visit this tree we call the "Jeremy Tree." We've taken many photos at the Jeremy Tree to remind us of his birth!

On February 25, 1988, while in Chicago preaching at a church, I was given a note telling me that #5, Kristel Ruth, had been born. This sort of interrupted the service, as you might imagine! I would have liked to have been there for that birth, of course, but Kristel only gave them 38 minutes of warning, and I was about two thousand miles away.

It's certainly humorous to look back on all this and reminisce about Mally's exciting birth experiences. Why relate these birth stories?

Well, whether a child can have a quick birth like most of ours did, or it takes a day or so, we have to remember that training these children to understand that everyone needs to be born again (John 3:1–21) takes much longer and involves daily hard work and sacrifice. Parents need to understand how serious we need to be about training our children up for the rebirth process, so they, we pray, will be believers in the Lord Jesus Christ.

****

One of my pet peeves is the concept of "Bible stories." Parents and Sunday schools around the world are innocently teaching children what I call "Bible stories," normally illustrated with unrealistic childlike illustrations. Noah's Ark, for example, is typically shown as a beautifully drawn little overloaded boat showing animals with their smiling faces hanging out the windows. However, nearly all of these "arks" would potentially sink at the first sign of water, let alone the oceanic turmoil the true Ark faced during the Flood. Also, these chubby little boats are not even close to the size required to fit all the animal kinds on board. . . . I guess that's why the animals always have to poke their heads out of the windows!

Now some of you are probably saying, "Come on. It's okay, they're only kids!" The sad fact is that the statement is true! They are only kids — kids that are vulnerable, teachable, and open to influence from us and everyone else. Many don't seem to realize children are very impressionable and open to every influence from the world. They are susceptible to every destructive, Bible-doubting idea around. When we present God's Word as "stories" and illustrate them in a way that gives the impression they are a fairy tale, can a child differentiate between Scripture and *Aesop's Fables*? I don't think so. When will we start becoming serious about teaching our children biblical truth instead of biblical tales? Keep in mind that the world scoffs at the account of Noah's Ark and the worldwide Flood — such fairy tale-looking arks actually help them scoff.

My father carefully constructed a scale model of the real ark from the dimensions given in the Bible.

To me it is a beautiful piece of work, meticulously re-created and crafted. Dad certainly wanted to ensure that people understood that the content of God's Word could be trusted, and we need to do the same. Never present the Bible as anything less than it is: the living Word of God. The main point is that as we were taught content, we were also taught the trustworthiness of the content and that the content was real. Dad always reminded us that the message was from God and that the Bible dealt with objective truth.

Certainly, there is a place for children's stories, symbolism, and allegory in our training. The fictional works of C.S. Lewis and John Bunyan are excellent examples, but whenever you open the Bible, make sure that your children understand that the content of this book is real. What's recorded in the Bible is true history. When it comes to holidays, make sure that your children understand that there is no correlation between the reality of our Savior Jesus Christ and the fictional Santa and Easter Bunny, etc. We have never used Santa Claus in any part of our family Christmas celebrations so that we don't cause confusion in this area. And besides, there is only one who can be everywhere and see everyone and know their hearts! And that One is God!

Now devotions in our home when our kids lived with us were never perfect. We just called it "Bible time." The kids got used to it and came to love it. When they were little, we would start with a good picture Bible and tell them the history and details of what was going on in the pictures. As they got older, we would read to them from the Word, and then have them read to us. And as creation apologetics books became available, we would show pictures of dinosaurs and read about them from a creationist perspective. As they grew, it became more than just reading the Bible, it became a time to communicate a biblical worldview. Of course, we had an emphasis on apologetics and teaching the foundational importance of God's Word. Every time we had Bible time, it communicated that the Book we held in our hand was special — it was God's inerrant Word.

I do realize that everyone has to answer for their own sins. "For we must all appear before the judgment seat of Christ, so that each one may receive what is due for what he has done in the body, whether good or evil" (2 Corinthians 5:10). Just because we train our children the best we could ever possibly do is no guarantee of salvation for them. But it has been thrilling for us as parents to see the fruit of the Spirit in the lives of our children to whom we did our best to ensure we pass on that spiritual legacy.

They married godly spouses, and now we are seeing them do their best to pass on the spiritual legacy to their children. But my wife and I will tell you that it has been hard work to impart this spiritual legacy. We didn't have polaroid kids spiritually — we had to put much time, effort, and prayer into their training. And really, it's never stopped — even after they've left home (though of course done in different ways as they've now "left father and mother")!

WELCOME
TO THE WAR

> *Be of sober spirit, be on the alert. Your adversary, the devil, prowls around like a roaring lion, seeking someone to devour. But resist him, firm in your faith. . . (1 Peter 5:8–9; NASB).*

❧

The family is under attack today like never before. The war on marriage, children, the family, and Christianity in general has really ramped up in the Western world. Wise parents need to recognize this and develop their own strategy for protection and counterattack. A generation is arising around us that knows not the things of God, allowing (and even encouraging) pre-marital sex, abortion, euthanasia, homosexuality, gay "marriages," pedophilia, gay clergy, and easy divorce. By and large, they do not believe there is such a thing as absolute truth or absolute morality. Not only is this degenerate generation arising, it already has arisen. These are the giants our children are facing. Generation Z is twice as atheistic as all previous generations and by and large has no concept of a Christian world-view. While a remnant of truth seekers remains, the attack on the family has the potential to eliminate Christian absolutes from our society as we are observing on almost a daily basis.

The attack is coming from those who build their thinking on the anti-God beliefs that are destroying society. This attack on the Word of God has resulted in the demise of the family unit — the very unit God uses to transmit the knowledge of Himself to each generation and the world. This is why it is so important we raise godly offspring who won't succumb to the evils of these giants. Yes, we need to train them to stand boldly and uncompromisingly on the authority of the Word of God.

The central issue in the battle is what people believe about origins, for these beliefs determine their worldview.

The attack on our kids is coming from several sources. Some of them are fairly obvious; others are right under your nose, and you probably don't even know it. Let there be no doubt that behind every attack is an enemy who is doing everything he can to covertly or overtly "steal and kill and destroy" (John 10:10). Satan is using a barrage of tactics to try to bring down your child and your family. Three of the most destructive are (1) secular humanism, (2) peer pressure, and (3) compromise.

Secular Humanism

"Secularism" is a philosophy that claims that there is no God — or that if there is a God, He is irrelevant. "Humanism" essentially says that in the absence of God, humans can and should act as gods by judging, choosing, and defining right and wrong for themselves. Actually, this is the essence of our sin nature. In Genesis 3:1–5, the devil tempted Eve by getting her to doubt God's Word by questioning, "Did God actually say...." He then said to her, "You will be like God...." In other words, you can be your own god and decide "right" and "wrong" for yourself. That's exactly what is permeating the culture more and more. In fact, a good way to describe the culture would be the way God's Word described it in the days of the judges: "In those days there was no king in Israel. Everyone did what was right in his own eyes" (Judges 21:25). In other words, when there's no absolute authority, everyone does what is right in their own eyes.

The philosophy pervading the public education system combines two philosophies into one — one that teaches that there is no God, that there are no absolutes, and that anything pertaining to the Christian worldview from the Word of God cannot be tolerated. And yes, we see a growing intolerance of the Christian worldview. This is the clash of worldviews — a secular worldview versus a Christian worldview.

The foundation of secular humanism in our modern age is Darwinian evolution — the religion of naturalism. That is why naturalistic evolution and dating the earth to be millions of years old is pushed so much in public (government) schools and other educational institutions today. Darwinian evolution and claiming that the earth is millions of years old are more than just issues of biology and age dating. At their very core is the philosophy that man, by himself, determines truth about origins and therefore life. That everything came into existence by natural processes. No supernatural is involved. Many don't understand this because they haven't been taught the difference between observational science (what one can observe and repeat — the science that built our modern technology) and historical science (beliefs about the past [e.g., origins] that cannot be directly observed or repeated).

Secular humanist philosophy has also infiltrated Christian institutions — those that have compromised God's Word with the world's teachings, for instance, by taking man's fallible ideas about origins and reinterpreting Genesis. They are training generations of students to believe the Bible is not infallible and therefore cannot be the absolute authority of God. In fact, they are really teaching that man's word is in authority over God's Word! The result should not be surprising, but it is still staggering: Barna research found that of the teenagers today who call themselves born-again Christians, only nine percent believe there is such a thing as absolute moral truth![1] Remember, earlier we learned Barna's 2018[2] research into generations and their worldview found the following staggering results:

1.   Barna Research Online, "The Year's Most Intriguing Findings, from Barna Research Studies," December 12, 2000, www.barna. org/cgi-bin/PagePressRelease.asp?PressReleaseID=77&Reference=E&Key=moral%20truth.

2.   *Gen Z: The Culture, Beliefs and Motivations Shaping the Next Generation*, Barna Group Report Produced in Partnership with Impact 360 Institute, 2018.

What about Gen Z?

The percentage of people with a biblical worldview declines in each generation.

Boomers—10%   Gen X—7%   Millennials—6%

Gen Z—4%

If you don't think the pressure is intentional or strategic, consider this 1983 quote from an American humanist:

> I am convinced that the battle for humankind's future must be waged and won in the public school classroom by teachers who correctly perceive their role as the proselytizers of a new faith: a religion of humanity that recognizes and respects the spark of what theologians call divinity in every human being. These teachers must embody the same selfless dedication as the most rabid fundamentalist preachers, for they will be ministers of another sort, utilizing a classroom instead of a pulpit to convey humanist values in whatever subject they teach, regardless of the educational level — preschool day care or large state university. The classroom must and will become an arena of conflict between the old and the new — the

rotting corpse of Christianity, together with all its adjacent evils and misery, and the new faith of humanism.[3]

Whether in public schools, Christian schools, or homeschools, parents must be aware of the influence teachers, textbooks, and other students have on their children. Non-Christian teachers without Christian convictions certainly cannot train their students in Christian truth. Because children under such teachers are trained with an anti-God and naturalistic evolutionary worldview, sinful temptations are often introduced through sex education, philosophy, and materialism. Because of their children's inherent tendencies (our sin nature) toward evil and away from God, parents must be even more diligent at home to refute the influences of secular humanism.

Peer Pressure

Do not be deceived: "Bad company ruins good morals" (1 Corinthians 15:33).

I believe peer pressure is one of the most effective weapons Satan aims at your children. It's a

---

3. John Dunphy, "A Religion for a New Age," *Humanist*, Jan–Feb 1983, 26.

huge pressure on us as adults as well. The bad will influence the good more than the good will influence the bad. This is a scriptural principle, and it makes obvious sense to anyone who understands the sinful tendencies of the fallen nature and the desires of the flesh.

Look at the example of Lot in Genesis 18 and 19. Did the evil in the city of Sodom influence Lot or did Lot influence Sodom for good? His sons-in-law didn't even believe him concerning God's warning that he was going to destroy the city! Even his wife looked back (longingly), contrary to God's clear instruction, and was turned into a pillar of salt. Think about it — who really influenced whom?

Let's be honest. When in a pagan environment, do our children bring home swear words and "dirty" jokes or do the others take home the Bible verses? Which is more likely to occur? You know the answer — the former is much more likely to happen. This takes place on all levels, from individuals to entire nations. Remember what Jeremiah said to the people in Jeremiah 10:2: "Thus says the LORD: 'Learn not the way of the nations. . . .' "

The Israelites were supposed to be influencing the nations, but instead they were constantly accepting the pagan ways of the nations around them, causing great problems and strife in their nation.

Over the years, we have sometimes been criticized as a family because we have been very cautious about whom we let our children mix with. We have been as careful as we could be to choose the children and adults with whom our children associate.

Many years ago, a youth group leader in our church wanted our children to attend in order to be a good influence on the others (who didn't have the same sort of biblical standards we did). The problem was, we didn't really want our children mixing with some of those others who might influence them for bad. We didn't think at that stage our children were mature enough to handle the situation, and so we had to make some tough decisions and limit our children's involvement in things that were even labeled "Christian." And we were criticized for doing this. But to us, in this situation, we had to put God's Word and our children first, regardless of the peer pressure from other adults!

Just because something is supposedly "Christian" doesn't mean it's safe. Many times, desperate parents will send a wayward child into a Christian school, or to camp, or to youth group, hoping that they will get "fixed." Ignorant parents also send innocent, God-fearing kids into these same environments and forget about their responsibilities to protect and train their kids, thinking they will be "safe" because it's a "Christian" environment. The mix can be dangerous, as it is much easier for our children to be dragged down than for them to drag the others up.

Mally and I had to deal with "peer pressure" issues on many occasions, and we always tried to do it in a way that would set a good example for our children to learn, for their future role as parents.

For example, one of our daughters (when about 12 years old) came home and said she was invited to a birthday party and a sleepover at the home where the party was to be held. She said a number of other young people would also be at the party and sleepover.

My wife and I were immediately concerned about who else would be at this sleepover and who would be supervising the event. In such an environment, we realized that peer pressure from others could have a negative effect on our children — and could lead to all sorts of problems, depending on who was present, etc. We knew that young people who didn't have the standards our family were used to could apply pressure to others to get involved in immoral activities, whether that be watching certain things on TV, viewing magazines, or certain immoral behaviors.

We told our daughter we needed to check things out carefully for her own protection. We called the family hosting the party and asked for more details about the event and the children who would be attending. We did not know this family well but understood they were members of a church. We then called their pastor and explained the situation to him. The pastor did not divulge confidential information but advised us to allow our daughter to go to the party, but certainly not to stay on for the sleepover. He had some serious reservations in regard to this.

Our daughter was told we would take her to the party and then pick her up at a particular time. I remember her being very disappointed. She tried to push us as parents to let her stay over — but we firmly and lovingly stood our ground. She went to the party and had an enjoyable time.

The next day, after she spoke to some of the others who stayed for the sleepover, she came and said to us, "I'm so glad I didn't stay for the sleepover. From what the others have told me, it was not good at all — it would not have been right for me to be there."

Lesson learned! And a child trained and protected as we believe should have happened in accord with our responsibilities before the Lord.

Remember also that children are not miniature adults. In this world of no absolutes, evolution, sex outside marriage, humanism, homosexual propaganda, and false religions — they will easily be tossed to and fro. They need to know how to recognize the difference between good and evil and choose the right way of thinking before being put under the pressure.

This creates a dilemma for those in charge of Christian schools, camps, and youth groups that involve non-Christians as well as Christians who have not been trained with a real biblical foundation. As a group, they seek to reach out to the lost, but the very people that they are trying to reach can put peer pressure on others to drag them down. This needs to be understood so systems can be put in place to deal with such a situation.

Compromise

We should expect attacks from the world, but often the attacks come at us from those who should be upholding the Word of God but are not.

That's called compromise. Compromise produces people who do not see God's Word as infallible. After generations of compromised teaching, many in the church end up not building their thinking on God's Word but form their worldviews on man's opinions. Many in the church don't understand the seriousness of this issue. Please understand this: Allowing a man-centered system (fallible, sinful man determines truth about origins) unlocks a door for others to consciously or unconsciously use a man-centered approach to the Scriptures in all areas. If man's ideas in biology, cosmology, and geology in relation to the past can be used to interpret Scripture, then it follows that man's ideas about morality can be used to interpret the Word of God in relation to the present. This is one of the reasons we see more and more churches agreeing with gay "marriage," supporting the ordination of gay clergy, defending abortion, or agreeing with sex before marriage, etc.

It's distressing that attitudes toward these and other unbiblical positions have softened to such an extent that many Christians don't even seem to know what is right or wrong concerning such matters. How sad it is that some of the very things that destroy the basis of the family are being tolerated in many churches and Christian schools, and even parts of our Christian home-education movement.

Tolerance of man's beliefs concerning origins and the age of the earth undermines Scripture and is in itself an intolerance of the authority of God's Word.

For example, the modern idea that the earth is millions of years old arose in the late 18th and early 19th centuries from the belief that the fossil layers had been laid down over a long period of time before man appeared. The fossil record is one of death (massive quantities of bones), disease (with evidence of cancer, brain tumors, abscesses, etc., in these bones), animals eating each other (with evidence of animal bones in the stomach contents of other animals), and thorns (supposedly 430 million years old). These beliefs are incompatible with the Bible's obvious teaching that death is an "enemy" (1 Corinthians 15:26), that animals were vegetarian before sin (Genesis 1:30), and that thorns came after sin and the curse (Genesis 3:18).

Darwinian evolution also teaches that humans arose from ape-like ancestors. However, this is incompatible with the Bible's record that the first man was made from the dust (Genesis 2:7, 3:19) and the first woman from his side (Genesis 2:22; 1 Corinthians 11:8).

Throughout the Scriptures we see God over and over again emphasizing the importance of accepting His Word as truth in passages such as Romans 3:4 which says, "Let God be true though every one were a liar. . . ." To compromise the Bible's clear historical account in Genesis with man's beliefs about the past is to compromise the very foundation of biblical authority.

Many Christians don't realize that they, their church, and the Christian colleges they support really are compromising and are thus tolerating destructive doctrine. It is very important to understand that Darwinian evolution and the popular belief that the earth is millions of years old grew out of philosophical naturalism. (I refer you to the publication *The Great Turning Point*,[4] by Dr. Terry Mortenson, for more information on this subject.)

Once the door to undermine biblical authority has been unlocked at the beginning (particularly in the Book of Genesis which is foundational to the rest of the Bible, to the gospel, and to all doctrine), it puts people on a slippery slide that can (and usually does) lead to a loss of biblical authority through the rest of the Bible. And such has contributed greatly to the exodus of the younger generations from the church in the Western world.

This brings up another very important factor to consider. Which college do you choose for your children? Perhaps a compromising Christian college may even be more destructive in some ways than a secular college where students can more easily discern the anti-God secular philosophies that they are being instructed in!

A California college student once told me she was going to a secular community college, but her science professor was an ardent biblical creationist. Also, she had been brought up on creation resources and had a solid stand on the authority of the Word and could defend her faith. She told me she had

4. Terry Mortenson, *The Great Turning Point* (Green Forest, AR: Master Books, 2004).

a friend whose parents sent her to an expensive Christian college. She said all her friend's professors at this Christian college believed in millions of years and evolutionary ideas — her friend was very confused and did not know what to believe about the Bible.

Even in "Christian" educational institutions, many do not accept God's Word in Genesis as literal truth. Most educators have been trained in the secular education system and often compromise truth without even really thinking about it. Many doubt and disbelieve much of Genesis — the 24-hour days of creation, the global Flood of Noah, the creation of Adam from dust, etc. — not because of what the Bible clearly teaches, but because of the acceptance of man's fallible ideas about origins and the age of the earth and universe. A significant number of Christians, including many in leadership positions, compromise with evolutionary ideas/millions of years, and thus compromise with secular humanism as well — since secular humanism is a logical outworking of such a foundation in fallible man's ideas. Because of this compromising contamination, the culture is not being built up, but is decaying instead.

It doesn't take an architect or engineer to appreciate the necessity of providing strong and secure foundations under any structure. If the foundation is compromised, total collapse is inevitable. We can easily see the structure of society collapsing on every side (particularly in the once very Christianized West). The hapless politicians certainly don't provide any long-term solutions. Sadly, and to our shame, much of the Church at large is also bereft of comfort and encouragement. The solutions offered by many seminaries have their basis not in the foundation of Genesis but in the humanistic, anti-God philosophy of Darwin and the atheists. Their philosophies have so permeated most churches (and therefore our society) that they are no longer good for much of anything.

If the Church does not emphasize this foundational aspect (teaching God as the Creator and the Bible's account of origins as true and refuting the anti-God belief that everything can be explained without God), then non-Christians will not be challenged. As long as they don't have to accept Genesis as true history, then they won't accept God's Word as the absolute authority — and ultimately, they won't have to accept any form of individual responsibility for their actions.

The compromise has actually trained generations in a philosophy like that of the Israelites in

Judges 21:25. This was the result: "In those days there was no king in Israel. Everyone did what was right in his own eyes."

That verse is an apt description of the Western world where we are now experiencing moral relativism permeating the culture as younger generations have been very secularized by the media and most educational institutions.

This condition logically follows from teaching that allows man's fallible ideas to reinterpret the clear words in Genesis. When compromise occurs, man has authority over the Scripture instead of God's Word being the absolute authority over man. It's nothing more than humanism in "Christianized clothing."

This man-centered philosophy is not something that occurred overnight. Generation after generation in the Church was permeated with these compromised positions. After years of indoctrination, each subsequent generation tended to have a lower view of Scripture, even though many did not realize this was happening. Great men of God who clearly were saved, sadly (and in many cases unwittingly) contributed to this lower view of Scripture because of their compromise with the world's ideas. Such compromise did not affect the salvation of these leaders, but it did affect how the next generation approached Scripture . . . and the next . . . and the next . . . resulting in that slippery slide that undermines all biblical authority.

These compromises need to be condemned because they destroy a literal Genesis and the basis of the family unit (since it is in Genesis that the family is established). They also destroy the foundation of a complete Christian worldview that integrates geology, biology, astronomy, anthropology, etc., because a true, scripturally based Christian worldview depends on the history in Genesis.

Now before we move on, we need to deal with an issue that crops up over and over again. When creationists take a strong stand that God created the earth six thousand years ago, they're often accused of making this a salvation issue. Well, it isn't a salvation issue — but it is!

Because Answers in Genesis and other biblical creationists take an authoritative stand on six literal (approximately 24-hour) days of creation and a young (approximately 6,000-year-old) age for the earth and universe, some have mistakenly taken our unwavering stand to mean these beliefs are salvation issues.

However, nowhere does the Bible even imply salvation in Christ is conditioned upon one's belief concerning the days of creation or the age of the earth or universe. For instance, Romans 10:9 states, "If you confess with your mouth that Jesus is Lord and believe in your heart that God raised him from the dead, you will be saved."

It does not state, "If you confess with your mouth the Lord Jesus and believe in your heart that God has raised Him from the dead, and believe in six literal days of creation and a young earth and universe, you will be saved."

Salvation is conditional upon faith in Christ — not belief about the six days of creation or the earth's age. So these are not salvation issues per se. But it is a salvation issue in an indirect sense. Let me explain. Many Christians, including Christian leaders, believe fossils, the earth, and the universe are millions or billions of years old. I contend that when they accept this timeframe and try to fit millions of years into the Bible, they are violating three vital issues.

An Authority Issue

One cannot get the idea of millions of years from the Bible. This idea comes from outside of Scripture.

When a Christian adds millions of years to the Bible and reinterprets the days of creation or tries to fit this extra time into the first verse in Genesis or a supposed gap between the first and second verses, he is allowing fallible man to be in authority over God's Word.

So, I assert that such compromise (which I believe it really is) is setting an example for others that fallible man can take ideas outside of Scripture and reinterpret God's Word to fit these in. Ultimately, accepting this view means God's Word is not the final authority and is not without error. It also opens the door to others doing this with other historical claims of Scripture — such as the Resurrection and virgin birth.

A Gospel Issue

Let me set this up with three major points.

First, Genesis 1:29–30 teaches that man and animals were originally vegetarian (before Adam's sin). How do we know this for sure? Humans weren't told they could eat meat until after the Flood in Genesis 9:3. This later verse makes it clear that mankind was originally vegetarian, but this changed after the Flood. Verse 30 of Genesis 1 (about animals' diets) is worded in the same way as verse 29 (man's diet), so it makes sense that originally the animals were vegetarian, too.

Second, at the end of the creation week, God described everything he had made as "very good" (Genesis 1:31).

Third, Genesis 3 makes it clear that the animals (v. 14) and the ground (v. 17) were cursed. And verse 18 makes it clear that thorns came into existence after sin and the curse: "Thorns and thistles it [the ground] shall bring forth for you."

Now the idea that things have been around for millions of years came from the belief that the fossil record was laid down slowly over millions of years, long before man's existence. So when Christians accept millions of years, they must also accept that the fossil layers were laid down before Adam — before the first human sin.

Yet the fossil record contains fossil thorns — claimed by evolutionists to be hundreds of millions of years old. How could that be if thorns came after Adam's sin?

The fossil record also contains lots of examples of animals that ate other animals — bones in their stomachs, teeth marks on bones, and so on. But according to the Bible, animals were vegetarian before sin.

Also, as discussed earlier, the fossil record contains examples of diseases, such as brain tumors, cancer, and arthritis. But if these existed before man, then God called such diseases "very good."

Taking all this into consideration, it seems obvious that bloodshed, death of animals and man, disease, suffering, and thorns came after sin. So the fossil record had to be laid down after sin, too. Noah's Flood would easily account for most fossils.

But what does this have to do with a gospel issue? The Bible calls death an "enemy" (1 Corinthians 15:26). When God clothed Adam and Eve with coats of skins (Genesis 3:21), a good case can be made that this was the first death — the death and bloodshed of an animal. Elsewhere in Scripture we learn that without the shedding of blood there is no remission of sins (Hebrews 9:22), and the life of the flesh is in the blood (Leviticus 17:11). Because Adam sinned, a payment for sin was needed. Because sin's penalty was death, then death and bloodshed were needed to atone for sin. So Genesis 3:21 would describe the first blood sacrifice as a penalty for sin — looking forward to the one who would die "once for all" (Hebrews 10:10–14).

The Israelites sacrificed animals over and over again as a ceremonial covering for sin. But Hebrews

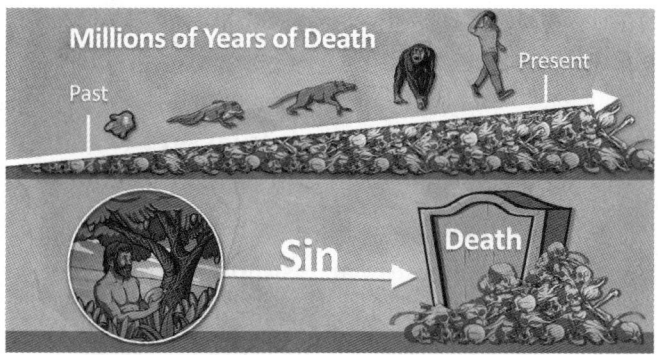

10:4 tells us that the blood of bulls and goats can't take away our sin — we are not physically related to animals. We needed a perfect human sacrifice. So, all this animal sacrifice was looking forward to the one called the Messiah (Jesus Christ).

Now if there was death and bloodshed of animals before sin, then this undermines the atonement. Also, if there were death, disease, bloodshed, and suffering before sin, then such would be God's fault — not our fault! Why would God require death as a sacrifice for sin if He was the one responsible for death and bloodshed, having created the world with these bad things in place?

One of today's most-asked questions is how Christians can believe in a loving God with so much death and suffering in the world. The correct answer is that God's just curse because of Adam's sin resulted in this death and suffering. We are to blame. God is not an unloving or incompetent Creator of a "very bad" world. He had a loving plan from eternity to rescue people from sin and its consequence of eternal separation from God in hell.

So, to believe in millions of years is a gospel issue. This belief ultimately impugns the character of the Creator and Savior and undermines the foundation of the soul-saving gospel.

An Indirect Salvation Issue

Many Christians believe in millions of years and are truly born again. Their belief in millions of years doesn't affect their salvation. But what does it do? It affects how other people, such as their children or others they teach, view Scripture.

Christians who compromise on the idea of millions of years can encourage others toward unbelief.

Their example can be a stumbling block to others. For instance, telling young people they can reinterpret Genesis to fit in millions of years sets a deadly example: they can start outside Scripture and add ideas into Scripture.

I suggest that such people can, over time, get the idea that the Bible is not God's infallible Word.

This creates doubt in God's Word — and doubt often leads to unbelief. Eventually they can reject Scripture altogether. Since the gospel comes from a book they don't trust or believe is true, they can easily reject the gospel itself.

So, the age of the earth and universe is not a salvation issue per se — somebody can be saved even without believing what the Bible says on this issue. But it is a salvation issue indirectly. Christians who compromise on millions of years can encourage others toward unbelief concerning God's Word and the gospel. God calls us to a higher standard in which compromise cannot be tolerated. There is no such thing as neutrality, as Jesus makes clear in Matthew 12:30: "Whoever is not with me is against me, and whoever does not gather with me scatters."

Scripture also makes it plain that if one is not walking in "light," then the only other option is "darkness" (see 1 John 1).

When secular schools in the United States (and similarly in the rest of the Western world) eliminated creation, the Bible, and prayer from the classroom, they didn't eliminate religion; they eliminated Christianity and replaced it with the religion of naturalism. Such a religion is not "neutral," it is anti-God. Millions of students are being trained to believe that humanity can explain every aspect of reality without God — this is "darkness," not "light."

In Revelation 3:15–16, the Lord told the Laodicean church that He would rather they be either hot or cold. Christ gives them this solemn warning: "So, because you are lukewarm, and neither hot nor cold, I will spit you out of my mouth." If we are "cold," we aren't affecting anyone; if we are "hot," and declaring biblical truth, then we are doing great things for the Lord. As soon as we compromise, we begin to cool, and then we begin to destroy — hence our Lord's stern rebuke.

As we train our children, we must take a stand for the Word of God and condemn error when necessary. This is something my father was an expert at! I recall the time my father received a daily devotional book from his church. He read the devotion on Genesis 6 and found that it claimed Noah's Flood was just a local event. This made him very upset. He immediately sat down and wrote a letter to those responsible for the devotional and showed them clearly from the Scriptures that Noah's Flood was a global event. He then went to the deacons at church and challenged them to stand up for the Scriptures and to rebuke those who wrote the material that undermined the authority of the Word of God and make sure the congregation knew this section was not correct.

On another occasion, a pastor during a sermon in church told us that the miracle of the feeding of the 5,000 could be explained this way: The little boy took out his loaves and fishes and thus set an example for the crowd, causing others to take their food and share with others. I could feel the heat steaming out of my father while he sat in the pew.

After the service, we immediately went up to the pastor, and I watched my father show this church leader (lovingly but firmly) from the Bible that he had misled the congregation and had compromised the clear teaching of the Word of God.

On another occasion, the same pastor was preaching again on the feeding of the 5,000 (maybe to get back at my father) and told the congregation there was a great contradiction in the Bible. In Matthew chapter 14 there is an account of the feeding of 5,000, but in Matthew chapter 15 it states there were only 4,000. I knew what was coming next!

My father went up to the pastor once again and pointed at the Bible and then looked at the pastor saying, "Haven't you read the Scriptures? These are two different events! In Matthew 16:9–10 Jesus stated, 'Do you not yet perceive? Do you not remember the five loaves for the five thousand, and how many baskets you gathered? Or the seven loaves for the four thousand, and how many baskets you gathered?'" The pastor had no answer!

What an impression this made upon me. It was all a part of preparing me for the ministry of Answers in Genesis, for later I confronted the same pastor about the origins issue. He responded immediately by saying there was no problem accepting evolution and adding it to the Bible. He told me a Christian could believe in evolution as long as they believed God created. He went on to warn me about taking the Bible at face value, claiming that there are lots of problems with the text — thus, one certainly can't take Genesis as being literal.

As the pastor made these statements, I recalled the times my father had challenged him in regard to biblical authority. Seeing my father successfully defend the Christian faith against this pastor's compromised positions instilled in me the fact that I needed to trust my father's words rather than this pastor's and take a stand myself. My father also had for years researched what the liberal critics of the Bible were claiming and had taught us answers to these attacks on God's Word so we wouldn't be led astray by pastors like this. Boy, was that pastor relieved when the Ham family moved on!

Isn't it interesting how certain matters become indelibly impressed on our minds — even from our childhood years? I believe that observing my father stand up for truth time and time again in my teenage years was essential to the journey that led me to what is now a worldwide ministry.

Yes, Mom and Dad, the war on the faith and the family continues, and there is no room for retreat. When it comes to secular humanism, peer pressure, and compromise, things are either for Christ or against Him. There is no in-between.

"Protect and Serve"

Many local police departments in the United States have adopted the motto To Protect and Serve. The sad thing is that most fathers are neither protecting nor serving their families and have not obeyed the Scripture's command to be the spiritual head of the house. Fathers one day will stand before their Creator God and answer why they did not spend the time to ensure their family was built on the Word of God as it was meant to be.

Most parents have left the training of their children to churches, schools, or colleges. Many think that they can be absolved because they have spent much money sending their children to Christian institutions, but again, relegating responsibility is very unwise. More and more we see forces at work in our society that take our children at younger and younger ages to train them in anti-God philosophies. In effect, this is producing a non-God-fearing, anti-Christian nation.

Each of us should also ask ourselves whether we are among those who have compromised with the world, rejecting a literal Genesis, and thus helping to destroy the backbone of the nation — the Christian family. Each father needs to be obedient to the Scriptures and ensure that his children are trained in the truth of God's infallible Word. I'm reminded of what the great reformer Martin Luther had to say:

> Wherefore, see to it, that you cause your children first to be instructed in spiritual things, that you point them first to God, and, after that, to the world. But in these days, this order,

> sad to say, is inverted. . . . In my judgment
> there is no other outward offense that in the
> sight of God so heavily burdens the world,
> and deserves such heavy chastisement, as the
> neglect to educate children.[5]

Parents who are engaged and proactive are highly important. I know this firsthand. Beyond the sovereignty of God, the influence of my parents was the only thing that kept my faith alive during the years I was immersed in public education. When I grew up in Australia, we had never heard of homeschools or Christian schools — they came years later.

All of my "secular" elementary education was completed at schools where my father was the principal. In his day, there was almost complete freedom to promote Christian teaching. At the beginning of each day, the whole school would assemble. When we lined up and various announcements were given, my father made sure that we always started with a prayer. On entering the classroom, each class would have readings from the Bible. My father also employed discipline

5. Martin Luther treatise, Letter to the Majors and Alderman of all the cities of Germany in behalf of Christian schools.

based upon biblical principles — and of course his Christian philosophy in every area pervaded his style of administration.

Because of my father's Christian character, he had a restraining influence on the whole school, which in the smaller rural areas affected the culture in the community, too. He applied God's principles in what he did as a school principal, and this permeated through the whole school, even though it was part of the secular education system.

Even under his leadership though, students were really learning secular concepts in geography, history, science, etc. As committed as he was, my father did not have a fully developed Christian worldview based on Genesis and the rest of the Bible as we have been able to do today. Later in life, as more and more creationist resources were published, he began to clearly understand this. Years later, I too began to understand how secular I was in my thinking in many areas.

I firmly believe that the influence of my parents and the restraining influence of my father's philosophy in elementary school greatly contributed to my spiritual survival. In regard to moral and spiritual matters, there is no doubt that many students, including myself, adhered to God's principles.

When I began high school in grade eight, however, it was a very different situation. There was no Christian philosophy permeating the school. The new textbooks were becoming blatantly evolutionary and clearly atheistic. I had to cope with an increasing number of students mocking me because I went to church. In many ways I began to struggle. I began to hear students talking about parties where they were involved in sexual promiscuity. Others would tell off-color jokes. The peer pressure was enormous. I spiritually survived, but only just. College was difficult as well, but because I lived at home, I really wasn't a part of the college environment. Still, there were a number of students who would attack my Christian stand on things.

My younger brothers will attest to the fact that when they went through public school (mostly after my father had retired due to ill health), there was no restraining influence as I had. They were also schooled in one of the bigger cities where things tended to be much less conservative than the more rural areas where I was brought up. (This is even true today in the United States or Australia — rural areas tend to be more conservative, and sometimes there can be a good percentage of Christian teachers who can also have that restraining influence.)

My brother David tells of the immense struggles he had at school and how he succumbed to the peer pressure to be part of the crowd. What a blessing that years later he was able to put that behind him and rededicate his life to the Lord. Of course, such actions aren't without their consequences, and to this day there is much regret.

Matthew 7:13–14 talks about there being a broad way to destruction and a narrow way to eternal life with God: "Enter by the narrow gate. For the gate is wide and the way is easy that leads to destruction, and those who enter by it are many. For the gate is narrow and the way is hard that leads to life, and those who find it are few."

I think most parents have a wrong understanding of this teaching. Many of us think of Christians being on one road that represents the narrow way, and that there's a separate road representing a broad way that non-Christians are moving on. Paul makes it clear in passages such as Philippians 2:15, "that you may be blameless and innocent, children of God without blemish in the midst of a crooked and twisted generation, among whom you shine as lights in the world."

The point is that Christians live in the same world as the non-Christians. In reality, the narrow way is within the broad way, going in the opposite direction. Most are on the broad way to destruction, sweeping along everyone else with them.

It takes a lot of work to drag our children in the opposite direction against the tide because we have to work hard against the sin nature, the natural desires of the flesh, secular humanism, peer pressure, and compromise. How successful we are at this very much depends on how much we have saturated our children's souls with the truth of God's Word and modeled for them an authentic relationship with Christ.

Hitler proved that if the children could be controlled for a generation that he would own the nation: "He alone, who owns the youth, gains the future!" This should make fathers and mothers more diligent in ensuring that their children are trained totally in the Scriptures, recognizing it as the absolute authority in all matters of life and conduct.

The bottom line, of course, is that this is an ungodly world and there is no perfect situation in which to raise godly children. However, the more parents understand biblical principles and what constitutes a truly Christian worldview, the more they will be able to discern the best things to be done in particular situations.

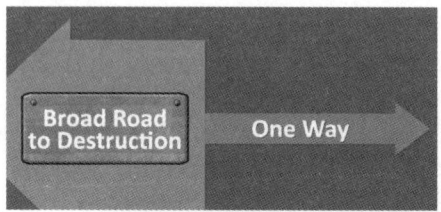

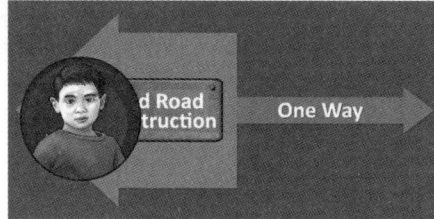

Parents, and particularly fathers, must be diligent in carrying out their God-commanded responsibility to train their children. There is no question about that. Foremost in the parent's mind must be that of creating an environment for sanctification that protects children from the immense pressures they face in the world. As you will see in the next chapter, that leads me to conclude that an excellent option for formal education takes place in the home, or at a carefully selected Christian school.

Key thoughts from this chapter:

1. Our children obtain their worldviews from their belief about origins. Some of the most destructive teaching in this area is right under our noses.

2. The teaching in our public school systems comes from an axiom of no absolutes and no ultimate truth. Teaching from this system has also infiltrated areas of the church, Christian school, and even homeschooling materials.

3. Just because something is labeled "Christian" doesn't mean it is safe.

4. Biblical discernment needs to be first taught to children as far away from an environment of ungodly peer pressure as possible. They need to know how to recognize the difference between good and evil and act upon the right way of thinking before being put under the pressure.

5. Parents should never underestimate the damage that secular and humanistic teaching can have on our children despite the environment they are learning in.

Building blocks:

1. Be on the alert.

2. Engage and get involved.

3. Monitor carefully the environment and the material that is influencing your kids.

4. Don't assume that something "Christian" is safe.

5. Condemn compromise.

Resources and tools:

Ken Ham, *The Lie: Evolution/Millions of Years.* (Green Forest, AR: Master Books, 2012).

Online apologetics courses from Answers Education Online. Visit AnswersEducation.com.

Terry Mortenson, *Millions of Years: Where Did the Idea Come From?* (Petersburg, KY: Answers in Genesis, 2005).

Terry Mortenson, *The Great Turning Point* (Green Forest, AR: Master Books, 2004).

CHAPTER EIGHT

VEGEMITE

KIDS

∾

One of the staples and delicacies of the Australian diet is a black paste called Vegemite. Made from yeast extract and salt, Vegemite is as standard in our diet as peanut butter is to the average American. Aussies like nothing better than to have Vegemite on toast with breakfast. We call it "savory"; Americans call it "hideous." Most Americans, when given Vegemite on toast, can't move fast enough to gulp down some water and get rid of what to them tastes horrible. Many compare it to chewing on bouillon cubes; one person claimed it destroyed his taste buds for six months! Hey, I know the stuff is salty, but it's not that bad!

So why do Australians crave Vegemite and Americans can't stand the taste of it? When I grew

up in Australia, mothers fed Vegemite to babies so they would learn to acquire a taste for this delicacy at a young age. Australians grew up loving Vegemite for the rest of their long and happy lives. Our kids are now training our grandkids to eat Vegemite from a young age.

Americans, however, don't get to taste Vegemite until an Australian suggests they try it — usually as

part of an ill-conceived prank. Because they have never acquired a taste for it, they can't stand it, and so will have nothing to do with it for the rest of their short and deprived lives. But the reverse situation exists concerning pickles. I wasn't brought up to like pickles, but most Americans are! I wasn't trained from a young age to like pickles — they are an acquired taste!

What then can we learn from this concerning the spiritual training of our children? Is there an analogy? With just a little stretch, I believe there is. Just like children need to acquire a taste for Vegemite at an early age, they need to be exposed to biblical input as well so that they might acquire a craving for the things of God, and the sooner they get this input, the more they will desire the truth throughout their lives.

Sometimes parents hold back on spiritual training until they think the child is "old enough." That is a big mistake and goes contrary to the biblical model. Think about these words written to Timothy from Paul in 2 Timothy 3:14–15:

> But as for you, continue in what you have learned and have firmly believed, knowing from whom you learned it and how from childhood you have been acquainted with the sacred writings, which are able to make you wise for salvation through faith in Christ Jesus.

It's never too soon to begin, and the more Scripture they are exposed to, the more they will absorb and become accustomed to the Word of God. As they learn to apply the truth that they are learning, they will develop the discernment to navigate through the temptations of the world, but this takes time and faithful feeding by the parents. Only as they mature will they be able to influence others in the same way. Consider this thought from Hebrews 5:14: "But solid food is for the mature, for those who have their powers of discernment trained by constant practice to distinguish good from evil."

When babies are born, they don't know about the Word of God. They don't know about Jesus dying on the Cross. They don't know what it means that God created in six days, and about marriage or any other Christian doctrine. When our first child, Nathan, was born, he didn't look up at me and say, "Hi, Dad! What are your views on eschatology and soteriology?" Without solid and continual feeding from the Word, all he would have would be the witness of a fallen creation (see Romans 1:19–20) and an unrefined conscience alerting him to basic right and wrong (see Romans 2:14–15). Our job as parents was to train him in that which is truth, so he could distinguish good from evil (Hebrews 5:14) and not be tossed to and fro by every wind of doctrine.

Children are NOT miniature adults!

Children are children!

Right from the time children are born, they need to be taught how to act and think as a Christian should. This means applying discipline in accord with biblical standards, having regular devotions and teaching times, practically applying Christian thinking in every area, making it clear that God's Word is central to the home, and protecting children from bad influences that they are not ready to handle. That's a given. We need "Vegemite kids" of faith, who will eventually long for the real meat of truth, and then become salt and light to the world. How will they stand against the anti-Christian giants if they're not trained for the battle as they should be?

The Great Education Debate

What about when it's time to begin formal education? We know that parents have full control and complete responsibility for training their small children, but what about after that? What is a concerned and engaged Christian parent to do when it's time for school? Most families have three options: 1) public (government) education, 2) private Christian schools, or 3) homeschooling.

It is my contention that while children are still maturing, godly training cannot happen in a secular education system or a compromising Christian one. Personally, for our children, we chose a combination of homeschooling and Christian schooling, with our last three children having been totally homeschooled.

Mixed options may be available as well, as there are many Christian schools that provide infrastructure for homeschoolers to attend part time. I know that there are exceptions to every rule, but they are just that — exceptions. I also know that circumstances may make the better choices impossible, but in general, according to the true ability and resources of the parents, true Christian education is what needs to be strived for.

Homeschooling has a long history in society and has existed to a greater or lesser degree in most cultures. In the last few decades, more and more families are choosing this option for their children. As the movement has grown, so have the support structures, materials, and curricula that are available. In most cities, parents can network together with other parents of like mind and values, sharing resources, expertise, and experiences — all of which can help keep costs down and improve the quality of the child's education. But some homeschools still use mostly secular texts and don't teach a truly biblical worldview.

Solid, biblically based Christian schools exist in certain communities. The cost is sometimes prohibitive, and as we've warned earlier, just because they are labeled "Christian" doesn't mean that the faculty or the curriculum upholds the authority of God's Word to the highest standard, nor does it mean that your child won't be rubbing shoulders with students who will be a negative influence. Many Christian schools use secular textbooks and really only attempt to Christianize a secular worldview. Only a minority of Christian schools seem to teach a true creationist biblical worldview.

When it comes to public education, which is based in secular humanist philosophies, the Christian parent would be wise to heed the words of the great reformer, Martin Luther:

> I would advise no one to send his child where the Holy Scriptures are not supreme. Every institution that does not unceasingly pursue the study of God's Word becomes corrupt. Because of this we can see what kind of people they become in the universities and what they are like now. Nobody is to blame for this except the pope, the bishops, and the prelates, who are all charged with training young people. The universities only ought to turn out men who are

experts in the Holy Scriptures, men who can become bishops and priests, and stand in the front line against heretics, the devil, and all the world. But where do you find that? I greatly fear that the universities, unless they teach the Holy Scriptures diligently and impress them on the young students, are wide gates to hell.[1]

Some feel that the influences of a pagan education can be offset by being part of a strong church, but this isn't enough. It is a known fact that with each passing generation, greater percentages of teenagers brought up in the church abandon Christianity. Over 90 percent of students from church homes in the United States attend secular schools.[2] Barna research reported that 70 percent of these students plan on leaving the church after they finish school.[3] Those statistics should wake up any parent who desires to raise godly children in this ungodly world.

1. Martin Luther, *To the Christian Nobility of the German Nation Concerning the Reform of the Christian Estate, 1520*, trans. Charles M. Jacobs, Rev. James Atkinson, The Christian in Society, I (James Atkinson, editor, *Luther's Works*, Vol. 44, 1966), 207.

2. Daniel J. Smithwick, *Teachers, Curriculum, Control: A "World" of Difference in Public and Private Schools* (Lexington, KY: Nehemiah Institute, Inc., 1999), 11.

3. Ibid.

I attended public schools and a secular university. Looking back at it all, I realize that the only reason I survived the system was because of the phenomenally unique convictions of my parents, the circumstances our family went through, and the times we lived in — and of course the Sovereign God who was in control of all situations.

If a parent must choose a public education for their children, they must be all the more diligent to train their children to gain the maturity to discern right from wrong. The parents have to be even more careful monitoring materials and teacher attitudes. Perhaps most importantly, the Christian student must have a mentality that reflects the reality that they are going into enemy territory when they go to school. Secular humanism dominates, peer pressure is intense, and "compromise" isn't even an issue — the system is now blatantly anti-God and indoctrinated by moral relativism and Darwinian thinking that by and large won't even allow the things of God, or even the possibility of a Creator, to be mentioned. The system is not their friend, and they must be aware and ready to defend themselves. Actually, I've found that the so-called "giants" who oppose Christianity largely only regurgitate what they've heard. Most have no idea how to even try to defend their ungodly positions. When godly generations are equipped with answers to defend their faith, they will stand against these giants and show them up as standing on the wrong foundation of sinking sand!

Forming a support group with other committed Christian students can help immeasurably with this. In the United States, because of the "Equal Access Amendment," students can now legally form on-campus Bible Clubs, prayer groups, and do limited group outreach. The restrictions on these groups can be significant, but it can be done, though increasingly secular schools won't allow such groups to exist as they claim they discriminate against those who support abortion or the LGBTQ movement. Of course, the reality is those schools discriminate against Bible-believing Christians who adhere to a worldview based on God's Word.

Mature Christian teachers can also be missionaries in the pagan public system . . . and they need our prayers because it is becoming more difficult to be light and salt in such situations. Adults ministering in this system are very different than immature students being trained by the system. Until a student has the maturity to discern right and wrong, and know how to diligently defend the Christian faith, the strength to stand up to peer pressure, and the determination to confront compromise, public schools can be a very dangerous place to be.

Keeping in mind that there could be restrictive legal issues in some countries, I stand by my recommendation that — as long as the parent has the ability and resources to do so — home-based education and carefully selected private Christian schools are the best options for educating Vegemite kids — those who acquire and desire the things of God.

Oppositional Arguments

It may surprise you that the main opposition I get for the educational choices my wife and I chose for our children (Christian school/homeschool) doesn't usually come from non-Christians, but from Christians!

The Salt Argument

Often, the criticism we get sounds something like this: "Your kids should be in the public school to witness to the other kids; you need to throw your children out into the world so they will learn to survive; they need to be mixing with non-Christian kids so they can be an example to them," and many other similar arguments.

When asked for biblical references for such a position, I often get an answer that goes something like this: "The Bible says we are to be the salt of the earth. Our children therefore need to be in the public schools so they can be salt and light to the other students." Now, it is true that Matthew 5:13 says, "You are the salt of the earth," but let's look at this passage in full context: "You are the salt of the earth, *but if salt has lost its taste, how shall its saltiness be restored? It is no longer good for anything except to be thrown out and trampled under people's feet*" [emphasis added].

Mark 9:50 states something else about salt that is very important and must be taken into consideration: "Salt is good, but if the salt has lost its saltiness, how will you make it salty again? *Have salt in yourselves,* and be at peace with one another" [emphasis added].

The point is this: A person can't be the salt of the earth until they have salt, and it needs to be uncontaminated salt that retains its saltiness.

Let's face it: Children are being contaminated as a result of their secular education, television, the books they read, and their friends. In a world of no absolutes, evolution, sex outside marriage, humanism, gay "marriage," transgenderism, abortion, the

LGBTQ movement, and false religions, children will be tossed to and fro.

How do they know which way to go? How do they know what to choose? They don't, unless they've been trained in truth and can recognize the difference between good and evil in the world . . . and as I've already said, I feel very strongly that this training is best done in the sanctifying environment where a true biblical worldview can be taught.

Because so many children from church homes have been trained by the government education system (which has become more and more anti-Christian over the years — to the point of eliminating Christianity totally), and because most fathers haven't really trained their children with a biblical foundation as they should, there are now generations of adults who attend church, but are so contaminated by the world that they think like the world. They lack salt, and the salt they have has lost its saltiness by contamination. These people then contaminate those around them and their own children. These children are often given no salt at all, or the little they have becomes even more contaminated than the parents' salt.

I believe that in many instances (not all, of course), what people call "teenage rebellious years" is due to a lack of being trained to acquire a taste for the things of the Lord in the early years. Once children become teenagers (and we all know that there are hormonal changes and certain behavior patterns related to puberty and adolescence), it is very difficult to change their behavior.

Contamination comes in many forms, but perhaps the saddest aspect is that much of institutional Christianity has compromised the Word of God, particularly concerning the doctrine of creation. Genesis (especially the first 11 chapters) is foundational to all Christian doctrine. Let me state my warning again: If generations are trained to disbelieve the Book of Genesis as literal history and to embrace man's fallible ideas concerning evolution and an earth that is millions of years old, they are put on a slippery slide of unbelief through the rest of the Bible. If the Bible's history is not accurate, then why should the Bible's morality be accepted? After all, the morality is based in the history.

The literal understanding of the events in the Book of Genesis is necessary to an understanding of what Christian doctrine is all about. Sadly, some children from Christian homes are being contaminated by what are called "Christian" schools. More and more schools are being established on secular humanism and a secular curriculum, to which God is added, but you can't Christianize a secular philosophy! You can't have both!

If you are going to opt for a private Christian education for your kids, don't assume anything when it comes to the content of the courses or the convictions of the faculty. Don't assume that the students there are going to be a positive influence on your children. Do your research on the school, monitor everything carefully, and never shirk your responsibility to be the one who trains your kid.

No matter what education you choose, know that you must be pouring the "salt" into your children — and this salt should be as uncontaminated as possible. Children need to be taught to acquire a taste for biblical teaching as early and as repeatedly as possible. Yes, we are all called to be "salt" to the world. Our children are to be this as well, but they must first be filled with pure salt from God's Word — leading to spiritual maturity and stability so that they can be missionaries

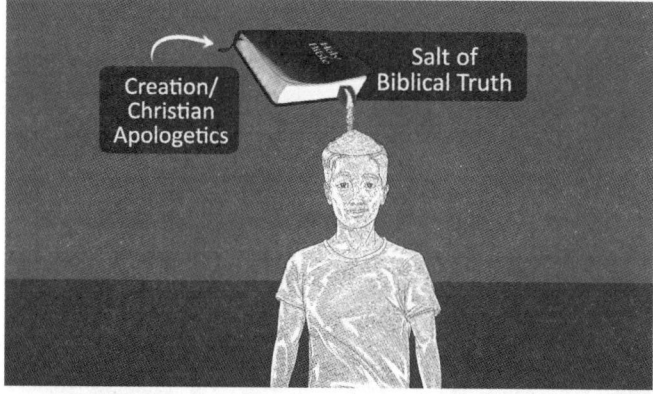

to the world without being contaminated themselves and made useless for the gospel. Children need the salt of biblical truth and creation/Christian apologetics so they can become mature adults being able to be salt and impact the world.

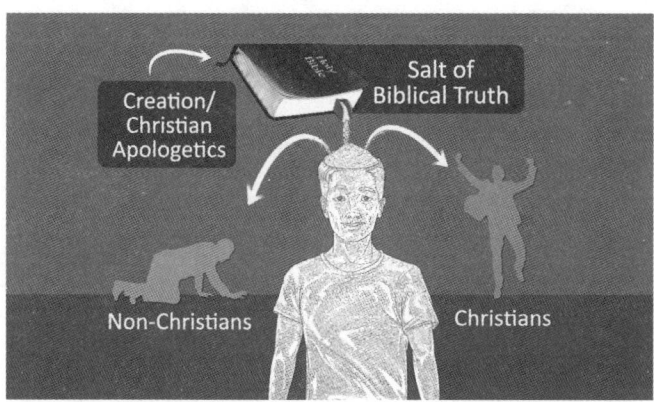

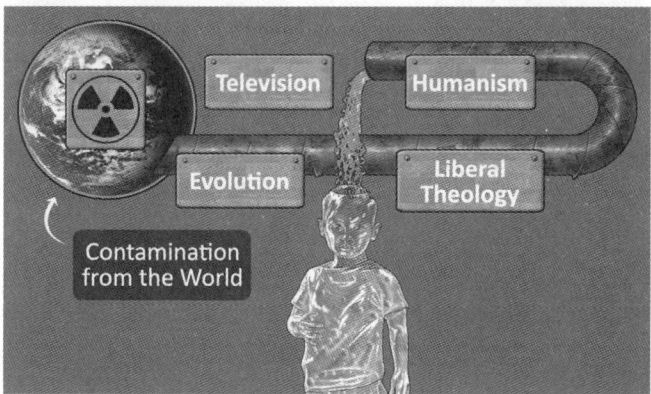

Good Kids

Some Christian parents justify their choice of public education by saying, "Yeah, but I've got good kids." Many child psychologists teach that children are basically "good" too, but the Bible teaches otherwise.

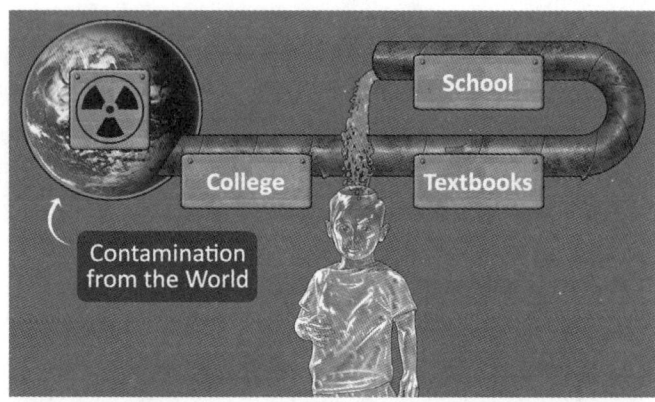

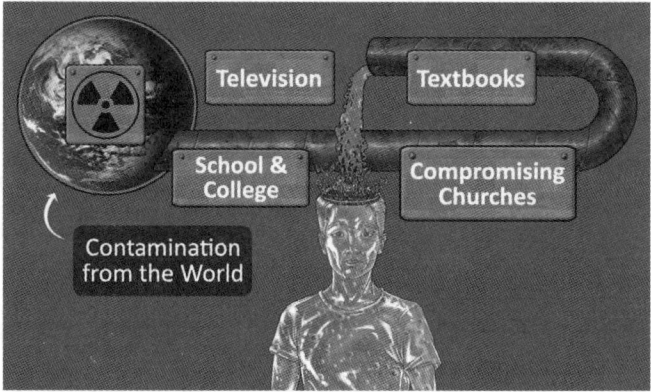

Psalm 51:5 states, "Behold, I was brought forth in iniquity, and in sin did my mother conceive me." Scripture tells us that children are a precious "heritage from the LORD" (Psalm 127:3) and that they are a great blessing in a Christian home. Nevertheless, children, like adults, must be viewed first of all as sinful creatures,

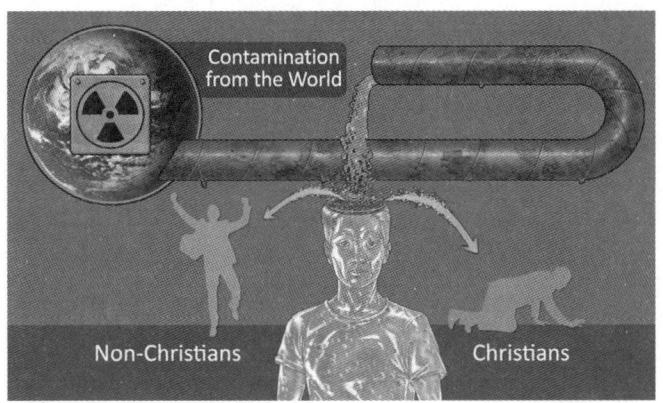

"For all have sinned and fall short of the glory of God" (Romans 3:23).

I remember visiting the hospital in Australia where my sister had just had a baby. I looked at this beautiful infant and said, "What a beautiful-looking sinful creature you have there!" I was thinking of Jeremiah 17:9 that says, "The heart is deceitful above all things, and desperately wicked; who can know it?" (NKJV). I was nearly thrown out of the hospital, as you might imagine, but when they took this baby home, it didn't take the parents long to find out I was right!

Because of the sin nature inherent in all mankind, and the natural desires of our flesh to do evil, none of us should ever think that we are "good" enough to be able to resist temptation. When placed in a compromising situation, we are more likely to be influenced by the bad than by the good. It's a challenge to get children to do what is right, but it is easy to let children do that which is wrong — just leave them to themselves, and they will express their true sinful tendencies.

Maturity comes with training, discipline, renewing the mind according to Scripture, and learning to walk in the power of the Holy Spirit rather than in the power of the flesh. That doesn't come naturally! It comes with maturity, and maturity takes time. Children are not miniature adults. They are unable to discriminate between good and evil. They don't have the discipline to choose between the truth and the cleverly crafted evolutionary philosophies.

Ephesians 4:14 states: "So that we may no longer be children, tossed to and fro by the waves and carried about by every wind of doctrine, by human cunning, by craftiness in deceitful schemes."

Paul also says in 1 Corinthians 13:11: "When I was a child, I spoke like a child, I thought like a child,

I reasoned like a child. When I became a man, I gave up childish ways."

The Bible makes it clear that children are easily led astray, easily tossed to and fro, easily deceived, and so on. Because of the sin nature and the flesh, a child in a pagan environment is likely to lose saltiness faster than gaining it, even if the parent is trying hard to fill the child with uncontaminated salt at home. (Consider how much time your children spend being trained in the pagan secular system compared to how much time they receive authoritative biblical input!)

Sadly, most children today are being contaminated by the world and compromised teaching in many churches and Christian colleges, and they grow to be contaminated adults impacting the world in a negative way.

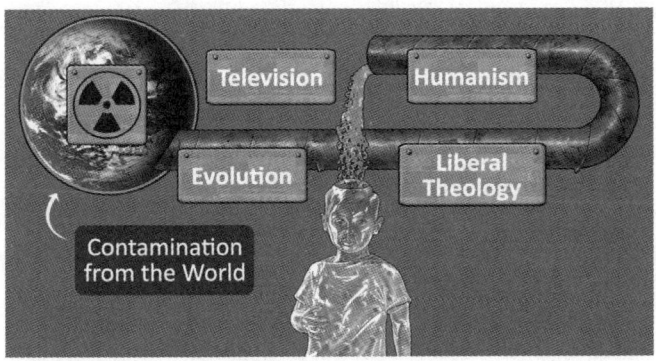

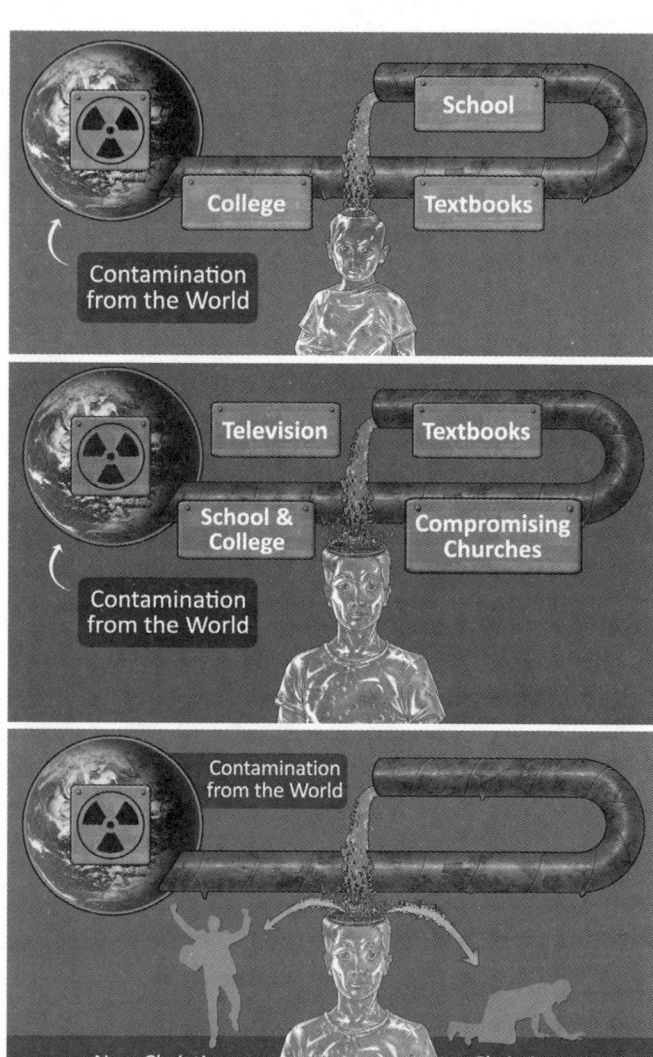

When the child becomes a man or woman, exhibiting spiritual discernment and biblical maturity, then they can maintain their salt and be salt and light to the world. Let's face it, when we as adults are given choices, our sinful tendencies draw us in the wrong direction. Would you rather read the Bible or a secular magazine? Are you more inclined to spend time praying or watching television? Would you rather go to a missions program at church or a football game at the stadium? If you have some extra money, would you prefer to buy Christian books or support Christian causes or missionaries or collect a new piece of furniture or new car?

I'm sure we all get the point. It's not that we shouldn't read magazines or buy a new car, but we need to consider our priorities according to what the Bible says is important, and children who still have much maturing in the Christian faith are very unlikely to do this.

So, in a sense, what I'm saying is that the salt is more likely to pour out of the children rather than to be retained by them. One night, when our first-born was in upper elementary school, he came and said, "Dad, someone at the Christian school told a dirty joke today and I can't get it out of my mind." Yes, contamination sticks with us — it is hard to get rid of because our flesh and fallen nature attract it. If we've allowed a lot of contamination to fill up these "vessels," it is going to be very hard to "decontaminate" them. That's why parents need to work so hard to avoid as much contamination as possible, and that's why dads and moms have to work with much prayer, patience, and perseverance to ensure as much salt as possible stays in the "vessel." There also needs to be much remedial work that reminds children over and over again of biblical truths that continually instill in them a Christian worldview (and the more that happens, the more the culture as a whole will be influenced for good). These things are very difficult to do when the child is spending all day in an anti-God, Bible-denying, secular humanist-enforcing environment.

Because of the fallen world we live in and the desires of our flesh and sinful nature, it is impossible to avoid all contamination. There are no perfect parents on this earth. We need to be aware of this and do our best to limit the contamination as best we are able because our kids, as much as we might love them and adore them, are not "good."

Legalistic Concerns

Others object to my education recommendations

by saying, "Wait a minute! Don't homeschooling and Christian schools force Christianity down their throats?" Sadly, I have had people tell me from time to time that their parents harshly imposed Christianity on them, causing them to reject it. "I'm not going to force religion on my kids," they assert.

In every instance where I've talked to people who have been hurt like that, Christianity was imposed legalistically from the "top down" through pressure (and sometimes power trips), where the parent tried to make themselves the ultimate authority, rather than the Bible. When parents humbly start with the Word of God and build "from the foundation up," starting with the logical foundations of all the doctrine in Genesis, not trying to prove the Bible with science, but using the Bible as the foundation for a truly biblical worldview in every area, and how to defend the faith by giving them answers to skeptical questions of the age — then it makes a world of difference.

Christianity then is presented as a logical and defensible faith that makes sense of the world and is confirmed by real observational science, instead of what seems to be just a collection of opinions. This is how we need to teach our children — from the time they are born until the time of our death.

Parents are to train children in the truth of Scripture, giving no options. For a Christian, it is not that truth is the best policy (as if it were one of several acceptable alternatives), truth is the only policy. Children who are merely taught can hear other teaching and easily depart from the truth because of their sinful flesh and their bias against God as expressed in their fallen nature. Thus, to cause children to be influenced for good, much work must be done. We must diligently train them in truth, condemning error for what it is. In Paul's letter to the Ephesians, he brings up another element that reduces the risk of legalism. Consider verse 4:15: "Rather, speaking the truth in love, we are to grow up in every way into him who is the head, into Christ."

In 1 Corinthians 13:4–7, Paul describes this "love" in detail: "Love is patient and kind . . . it is not arrogant or rude. . . . it is not irritable or resentful. . . . Love bears all things, believes all things, hopes all things, endures all things."

I would propose to anyone who has legalistic concerns about education, that when the truth is taught in an environment of this kind of love, kids will never feel like Christianity is being forced upon them. In fact, the home is where children need to first experience this kind of love from the parent, even as they learn to fulfill the greatest commandment in all of Scripture, Deuteronomy 6:5–7:

> You shall love the LORD your God with all your heart and with all your soul and with all your might. And these words that I command you today shall be on your heart. You shall teach them diligently to your children, and shall talk of them when you sit in your house, and when you walk by the way, and when you lie down, and when you rise.

Even when homeschooling or a private Christian education seem like the best options, however, circumstances can make it impossible. Allocating the time and finances for homeschooling can be difficult for single-parent families. Many families depend on a dual income and still don't have enough for tuition at a private Christian school. In other situations, there might be disagreement between parents when either the father or mother is not a Christian. It's also possible that a solid Christian school doesn't exist in your area, or maybe you live in a country where homeschooling resources are very, very limited (or you live in a country where homeschools and Christian schools are illegal).

These are all serious struggles, and they reflect the fact that we certainly live in a fallen world where difficulty is a part of life.

If you are one of the people in this category, the fundamentals still apply. You may have to work harder than others and you may have to access more help, but you have the same responsibility to provide foundational scriptural instruction to your children. You have the responsibility to belong to a strong Bible-believing and teaching church, and you have the responsibility to manage the circles of influence that your children are exposed to. If you have no option but for your children to be educated in the secular system, then you must acknowledge that the responsibility of the position you hold has just been magnified, and therefore checking homework and monitoring your children's friendships, and teaching them how to have a biblical worldview and how to defend the Christian faith will be a vital part of your parenting. Always remember that it is your responsibility, within your means, to see that your child is trained and educated according to biblical principles.

God is a gracious God and forgives, but the consequences of your actions will still be part of the legacy you leave . . . and you only have one opportunity to leave it, so you better be sure you're doing it as you should. If God's people do not produce godly offspring, then the application of the truth of God's Word will be severely and negatively impacted for generations to come or to the world around. Who then will be our evangelists, pastors, missionaries, Christian teachers, Sunday school teachers, and godly parents?

In Summary

God's Word lays down principles about how to train children — the priorities and methods. So I would pose this question: If someone asked you right now to explain what God teaches regarding the nature of children, how to train them, the priorities for their education, and who is ultimately responsible, could you give an adequate answer? Now it's not possible in this short book to give all my answers, but you can watch one of the presentations I gave when my friend Dennis Rainey and I did a parenting conference in 2019 on Answers.tv. If you can't answer those basic questions, then whose methods are you using? Are they the right methods? (See *Raising Godly Children in an Ungodly World*.)

I've heard people use the reasoning, "I send my kids to public school because the Bible says we are to be salt" (Matthew 5:13). Yes, but the Bible also states we need salt in us (Mark 9:50). Matthew 5:13 also tells us that if the salt is contaminated, it's no good. So, parents (and particularly fathers as the spiritual head) have a responsibility to ensure that they put the salt of biblical truth in their children, teaching them doctrine and apologetics to defend their faith against secular attacks. They are to do their best to stop contamination by the world. The point is, children can't be salt until they have it — and if the salt's contaminated, it's basically useless.

If your kids are in public school, you can't ignore the fact that — by and large — they are being taught a secular (anti-Christian) worldview. This education system has mostly thrown out God, the Bible, prayer, and creation; students are taught how to explain everything by natural processes. But naturalism is atheism. There is no neutrality. We're either for or against Christ (Matthew 12:30; James 4:4). One has to recognize that public schools have become basically churches of atheism and moral relativism.

Finally, children are beings who are going to live forever and ever and ever and ever and ever . . . in heaven or hell. There is no greater invest-ment than in the eternity of our children. What an incredible responsibility we have as parents! So what principles are we using in training our children? Who really has the greatest influence in their lives? Yes, each person has to answer to the Lord in regard to whether they are saved or not. But are we doing the very best we can to take our children to heaven with us?

Only those children anchored in the Word of God, who know what they believe, why they believe what they do, and know how to defend the Christian faith and answer skeptical questions that attack God's Word will be able to survive the tornado raging around them. That's what matters for eternity.

But whatever gain I had, I counted as loss for the sake of Christ. Indeed, I count everything as loss because of the surpassing worth of

> knowing Christ Jesus my Lord. For his sake I
> have suffered the loss of all things and count
> them as rubbish, in order that I may gain
> Christ (Philippians 3:7–8).

Key thoughts from this chapter:

1. We cannot expect our children to be salt and
   light until they first become salt and light.
   It is too easy to lose saltiness in an unsalty
   environment.

2. It is impossible to train children under a
   worldly system and then add God to it. You
   cannot Christianize a secular philosophy.

3. Our children are not "good." They have sinful
   natures and fleshly tendencies that make
   them highly vulnerable to temptation and
   compromise.

4. Building a defensible biblical foundation for
   our children allows them to develop a defensible faith. When done in love, this is completely different from forcing Christianity on
   them from the top down.

Building blocks:

1. The educational choices you make have great
   impact on the sanctification of your child.

Make these choices wisely, according to biblical principles, and even at great personal sacrifice.

2. Always monitor the content of what your child is being taught, even in a Christian school or in homeschool curricula.

3. Never give up your responsibility to be the primary trainer of truth for your children.

4. Strive to always communicate the truth in love as described in 1 Corinthians 13.

Resources and tools:

Websites:

www.gocampus.com. Student Venture. Find everything you need to be a missionary at a secular school.

www.aclj.org American Center for Law and Justice. To find out your rights as a Christian at a public school, click "On the Issues" and go to "Equal Access."

www.christianlaw.org is another source of legal advice in schooling issues.

Homeschool Legal Defense Association at HSLDA. org.

www.thehomeschoolmagazine.com is the website

for The Old Schoolhouse magazine which is a good source of information on homeschooling.

Books:

Starting a Campus Club (Gospel Publishing House) www.youth.ag.org, 1-800-641-4310.

GENERATIONAL LEGACY

Author's Note: I thought it would very fitting for this book to give a practical example of the spiritual legacy being passed on to the next generation. I asked our eldest daughter, Renee, who founded a Christian school (Twelve Stones Christian Academy) under the auspices of Answers in Genesis, to write a chapter on her understanding of Christian education.

❧

EDUCATION…What Does the Bible Say?
By Renee Hodge

My personal story:

It's almost fitting that I ended up in education. Not only did my dad start out to be a science teacher, but his dad (my poppa) was a well-respected administrator through Queensland, Australia. The education system we have today has seen better years, and it's unfortunate where it has landed.

One of the main questions I get asked when people find out that I'm Ken Ham's daughter is, "What was is like growing up with Ken Ham being your dad?" Well, it was normal to me because that's all I knew! But I must say that my parents trained us up to have a passion for the authority of God's Word. Not only did they preach it, but they lived it as well.

At the age of 9 years old, we moved from my home country of Australia to America. My parents had sent me to a Christian school since kindergarten. Homeschool was not done in Australia at this point, so my parents did not even know that was an option. In America, my parents kept trying to find a good Christian school for me and my siblings and ended up in a different school almost each year. I remember being at one school for only 6 weeks and my parents yanked us!

I remember the struggle my parents had in finding a good solid biblical school. You see, if we are to take a stand on the authority of God's Word in all areas, then doesn't that mean education also? My parents sure sacrificed a lot to make sure that happened for us. Even for college, it was Christian education all the way.

When I had my first child, one of the early discussions with my husband was what school are we going to be sending our kids to? The only option was true Christian education. Government schools teach secular views in every subject — they think they are teaching a neutral position, but they are not. They are in fact teaching and actively promoting secular humanism, which is a religion that is in opposition to God's Word. Unfortunately, many Christian parents unwittingly send their children to government schools and don't realize the indoctrination and brainwashing that is occurring there to impose secular beliefs and values on unsuspecting students.

So, it was Christian education all the way for my kids. Some of my siblings homeschool, but for a number of reasons, we decided on Christian school for our family. We were looking for a Christian school that stood boldly on God's Word and taught every subject through the lens of the Bible while also giving them a high-quality education. And just like that I found myself in the exact shoes that my parents were in . . . trying to find a good biblical school for our children!

We live in an area that is dominated by Catholicism and secularism (the Cincinnati area was originally a German Catholic settlement) with few Christian school options — in fact, there are hardly any Christian schools in the area we live in. All I can say is that the Lord laid an intense desire on my heart to see a good biblical Christian school start up in this area, and He has helped guide me every step of the way.

The Bible talks a lot about training up the younger generation, leaving that godly legacy, and that is one of the most important things a parent can do for their children! Because of this, Twelve Stones Christian Academy (Joshua 4:21–24) was born in 2017.

Twelve Stones Christian Academy (TSCA) was started not just to be any Christian school, but a unique biblical worldview school. Here is what makes us unique (and most of this applies to homeschool too):

Biblical worldview: We begin with the Bible as the absolute standard and final authority in all subject matter, not just faith and practice. We are unashamed of this fact.

Solid biblical Christian curriculum with academic rigor: We don't just pick any Christian curriculum but are very meticulous in searching for the right curriculum that fits our mission for biblical worldview, critical thinking skills, and academic rigor.

Critical thinking skills: We want to train up our students to think logically and critically in all areas — this is also incorporated into the curriculum, and in addition, we have logic classes for middle school and high school to be able to spot logical fallacies and errors in reasoning.

Statement of faith: We have a solid in-depth statement of faith that that lays out biblical apologetic and worldview doctrines in detail that guide the school to keep it on course.

Discipleship focus: We don't take just any family, but those families that are like-minded and want to disciple their children. I think it's great that there are Christian schools out there that bring in many non-Christian families in an effort to evangelize. The problem with this is that they presume the other Christian students there are up to the challenge of influencing the "rotten eggs" by being fluent in the Bible already, apologetically sound enough to refute the arguments, and able to stand up against the secular peer pressure. Let's be honest, these kids aren't up to the task of being biblical and apologetics experts yet at this level because they themselves haven't been fully trained yet. Isn't that why they are at a Christian school? We know very well what happens to a rotten apple in a basket of good apples . . . the bad influences the good.

Parent partnership: Our school exists to partner with parents and be an instrument to assist in providing a Christ-honoring education that is biblically, academically, morally, spiritually, and relationally sound. We have parent communication as a top priority, so they know exactly what their children are being taught.

Well-thought-out Bible program: So many schools leave Bible class up to the particular teacher with minute thought to a scope and sequence. Plus, many Bible classes are an "easy A," which subtly passes along a message that the course is largely irrelevant. Sadly, if a day needs to be shortened or a teacher needs more time for something, it's the Bible class that gets chopped. Our Bible program is a well-thought-out program to deal with apologetic topics and cultural issues while training the students in biblical and scriptural truth with significant memorization and application. Each Bible class builds upon the previous year, so by the time our kids are in high school they are at a level that is well beyond most adults in today's Christian culture. It's also a class they need to work and study hard for just like any other academic class and is a priority for any given day.

As you can tell, our model of education is significantly different because we have a desire to properly train the kids in ways that have fallen short for decades within the church and much of the home-school and Christian school movements. Our goal is to take Christian education and build it into a structure with a solid biblical foundation without compromise, the way it should be done, just like every other area of our life.

Parents' Role in Education:

One of the most important decisions a parent can make for their children is where they will go to school. Over the course of K–12th grade, a child will spend roughly 16,000 hours in school compared to 700 hours at church — if you attend weekly and regularly. As you can see, what your child is being taught at their school will have a much more profound impact on them. So, what does the Bible say about the kind of education a child should receive?

Deuteronomy 6:6-7 states,

> And these words that I command you today
> shall be on your heart. You shall teach them
> diligently to your children, and shall talk of
> them when you sit in your house, and when
> you walk by the way, and when you lie down,
> and when you rise.

Ephesians 6:4 states,

> Fathers, do not provoke your children to anger,
> but bring them up in the discipline and in-
> struction of the Lord.

These verses show that it is the responsibility of the parents to seek to provide a God-centered and Christ-honoring education for their children. As Christians, the Bible is our authority in all areas, including education.

Some parents take this directive on themselves and homeschool their children, whereas others seek to partner with a Christian school to help them in this area. In either case, it is important to make sure that a solid academic and biblical education is given so that these children are prepared for "leaving the nest."

As a mom, it saddens me a little to think that I'm training up my kids to lead a successful, independent, and godly life apart from me. But that's exactly what our job is as parents! What a great responsibility. Hence, the decision of schooling must be taken with much seriousness and prayer.

Whatever schooling decision is made, there is always a sacrifice that must be made. I think of Christian schools and the financial sacrifice that parents make. Homeschool usually places a huge burden specifically on the mom (and sometimes her sanity!).

If there is a child in public (government) school, there must be many extra and intentional hours poured into the kids to counter the secularism (really atheism) that is being infused into them at school in every subject and virtually every textbook, which sadly doesn't get done in most instances. This is reflected in the fact that the majority of kids in church homes walk away from the faith. Far too often, the children are trained to be secularists, and there was very little to counter this education.

So, what is the ideal answer? Because we live in a sin-cursed universe, unfortunately, there is no perfect solution. We must seek the Lord in prayer and seek His Word and try to align the best we can with the kind of education God says we should be training our children with.

The Problem

Sadly, Christianity is under attack today, and the religion of secular humanism (and consequence of moral relativism) is dominant in our culture and taught in the public school system, secular media, secular museums, and secular textbooks. The ideas of gender neutrality, big bang, apelike creature-to-man evolution, atheism, moral relativism such as teen sex, homosexuality, anti-pro-life, etc., are bombarding our kids in this day and age and causing them to doubt the Bible. Most churches, Sunday schools, and youth groups preach sermons on spirituality and basics and often don't deal with cultural issues head-on, and apologetically combating the humanistic thinking that is being imposed on our unsuspecting children.

When most kids graduate from high school (whether homeschool, Christian school, and especially public school) and college, they are unprepared for how to defend their faith from the secular onslaught. Statistics reveal that about two out of every three kids in church homes are walking away from the faith, even as young as middle school and high school age, and very few are returning. This is what happens when you separate the Bible from education. Contrary to popular belief, secular education is not neutral.

What Is a Truly Biblical Worldview?

By and large, a child has developed their worldview by the age of 13. Simply put, a worldview is the way people view the world. It is essentially a religious viewpoint through which everyone looks at existence. Ultimately, there are only 2 worldviews: looking at the world through God's Word (the absolute authority), or if you reject that, then you default to man's word as the final authority, which is based on arbitrary opinion.

All authorities outside of Scripture are lesser authorities (a faulty appeal to authority fallacy). Scripture is supreme and profitable for doctrine, for reproof, for correction, for instruction in righteousness, that we may be complete, thoroughly equipped for every good work (2 Timothy 3:16–17). A biblical worldview stands against all other religions (whether secular humanism, Eastern mysticism worldviews, pagan worldviews, and so forth). It is a worldview that mimics the way God looks at His creation.

God's revealed truth is the Bible. It is the absolute standard to correct our thinking and understanding about God's world. It would be illogical to neglect God's Word when looking at the world. Thus, we presuppose God and His Word in an effort to understand basics about existence, logic, truth, knowledge, morality, science, and so on.

God is the basis for a biblical worldview, and as Christians, we strive to follow God's example. Education should implement a biblical worldview infused throughout the curriculum and every facet of school life (2 Timothy 4:2), using a biblical framework in mathematics, arts, history, sciences such as biology and physics, literature, logic, morality, personal relationships, missions, evangelism, and so on.

It's important that the curriculum that is picked is grounded in scriptural teachings from a biblical worldview, apologetically focused, and academically rigorous so that it will equip the students with skills and knowledge to defend their faith, become good stewards of God's earth, and be bold witnesses for Christ. Good Christian curriculum will also give students a chance to better understand the nature of God and to have a deeper appreciation of the world God designed for us that has been marred by sin. Sadly, the majority of Christian schools use mainly secular textbooks. Let's take a big-picture approach at how each subject is taught through a biblical worldview.

Mathematics is a unique language in which we can study and express abstractions of the physical world using logic. Everything in our physical world has features that can be measured and studied. When we isolate one or a few features for study, we see a reflection of God's nature: consistent, orderly, and logical. Only by the absolute standard of God do we have a basis to do mathematics. God gave us the ability to do math so that we may better understand Him and His creation and to obey His command to have dominion.

Science only works because God is upholding all things in a particular way and promises to continue to do so as long as the earth endures (e.g., Genesis 8:22). With God's Word we can understand geology in light of the Flood, astronomy in light of Genesis 1, biology in light of God's created kinds, etc.

We also use science and the Bible to help us understand evidence. Everyone has the same evidence . . . the same earth, rocks, stars, DNA, etc., but the difference is the interpretation of that evidence. There are only two choices: God or man. A biblical worldview is where you start with God and His Word to understand the evidence (i.e., the worldwide Flood caused most fossils and rock layers). If you reject God, then you are relying on man's fallible ideas and using that as your basis for looking at the evidence, which is trying to explain the world without God.

History starts in Genesis 1:1, "In the beginning God created the heavens and the earth." Therefore, there is no such thing as "prehistoric"! The Bible's record of history is inerrantly revealed to us by a perfect God. It is the absolute truth, and when the world's rewritten history deviates from God's Word, it is that alleged history that is in error. We oppose the false views of history that are being articulated in our culture. False history like molecules-to-man evolution, millions of years (geological evolution), evolution from ape-like creatures in an "out-of-Africa" model, and big bang are challenged with the truth of history that uses God's Word as the foundation. As kids learn the true history of what happened according to God's Word, they are better able to spot these common false claims and discern why they are wrong.

English — where do languages come from? Language was created by God so that we could communicate with Him and each other, but now we have a diversity of languages because of what happened at the Tower of Babel. Language families left Babel with various family groups being put to written script, whether pictorial, alphabetic, etc. Then languages continue to change — adding words, losing words, changing definitions, changing grammar, tonal adjustments, etc., to arrive at the various languages we have today (about 7,000 of them).

Logic — we are made in the image of a logical God who cannot deny Himself (e.g., 2 Timothy 2:13), and His creation is upheld up in a logical way, so this helps us be able to properly reason in every area.

Fine arts is grounded in the fact that we are created in the image of a creative and artistic God. When we do art, we are mimicking, in a small sense, what God did at creation.

Health/PE — since our bodies are the temple of the Holy Spirit (1 Corinthians 6:19), we need to take good care of ourselves in what we do to our bodies and put in our bodies.

The Bible course should be fully integrated and used as the basis for refutations of all false worldviews and false belief systems throughout all subjects. Even so, the students need an age-appropriate Bible class to help them understand biblical truth and knowledge. First and foremost, their heart should be the number one priority in coming to salvation through repentance and reception of the blood of Jesus. Only then can they form the right worldview to build all their thinking on (e.g., 2 Timothy 2:24–25).

We need to remember Proverbs 9:10, "The fear of the LORD is the beginning of wisdom. . . ." It is the role of every parent and educator to shape the worldview of their students, using the Bible as the authoritative guide, and to look at each subject through the lens of Scripture.

Let's not shy away from what the world is teaching so that we can refute it biblically and logically. The students need to know what is being taught in today's culture and why secularism (or any other religion) is wrong. By the time these children graduate high school, they should know what they believe, how to defend it, refute false religions, be bold witnesses for our Lord and Savior, and be prepared academically for the next step of vocational/career training.

Academic Rigor

Each student should be challenged at the appropriate grade level. Academic rigor should be done in a way that's not frustrating or overwhelming, yet it should push the child to continue to grow by learning and understanding while creating those critical thinking skills. In Colossians 3:23, it states, "Whatever you do, work heartily, as for the Lord and not for men." Just as we ask our children to do the best of their ability for the Lord, so should we in the education that we offer to them.

It grieves me when I see some homeschooled children that are far behind academically (anywhere from 1–2 grade levels behind). I see this in some Christian schools as well. Of course, there are many exceptions to this. But for some reason, there is a false view that is out there that if you're a Christian school your focus will either be Bible or academics. But this is a bifurcation fallacy (an either-or fallacy). You CAN have both, and the Lord calls us to have both! I applaud homeschool parents and these Christian schools that are trying to do their very best and provide a great Christian education, but you can't neglect the academics!

College After High School?

Phew! Your child has made it through 12th grade and is off to college (or vocational training). Unfortunately, so many children head off to secular (pagan) colleges and universities and don't survive that system. Most are just not prepared to try to survive. Just because someone is 18, now independent, and going off to college does not mean they are immune to the world's enticement of secularism — not even adults are immune.

The Bible warns all of us that we are in a spiritual battle (Ephesians 6:10–18) and we must walk in the spirit of God (Galatians 5:16). Going to school at a secular institution, the student will be studying based on secular humanism (where man is elevated as the authority) vs. studying with the Bible as our foundation (where God is the authority). In many cases, they will deal with anti-God professors and repeated attacks on God's Word. There WILL be a negative effect. The secular world will have an impact on the student, and is it worth it? There is no neutrality — you are either for God or against Him (e.g., Luke 11:23)!

Again, since the Bible is our authority in *all* areas, then it also must be at the college level if possible. Our children need to be trained and ready for the spiritual battle we are in. Even at the college age, most children are not yet ready but still very impressionable by their peers and college professors.

In the military, we don't send people into battle without properly training them rigorously, and this goes for our children as well. They cannot be the salt and light of the earth until they have been properly trained to be that salt and light (Matthew 5:13–16; Acts 13:47; Philippians 2:15). We need to understand that the world is out to turn our kids against God. James 4:4 states, "You adulterous people! Do you not know that friendship with the world is enmity with God? Therefore whoever wishes to be a friend of the world makes himself an enemy of God."

Is All Christian Education Equal?

The quick answer . . . no! I don't like to just ask if it's Christian because that could have multiple meanings depending upon whom you are speaking to. Just because a curriculum claims to be Christian or a school claims to be Christian, don't take it at face value — do your homework! I try to find out how biblical they are . . . is their program or curriculum built on a biblical worldview and integrating God's Word?

Some "Christian" schools presume they are Christian because they have a Christian charter that says so or that they offer a prayer to begin the day. But otherwise, they use and teach a secular worldview (with maybe God added somehow) throughout the day. Some "Christian" schools may also have a Bible class thrown in, but secular textbooks and compromised teachings (e.g., big bang, millions of years) still dominate. Some "Christian" schools have a "Christian" curriculum, but that curriculum does not adequately provide a truly biblical worldview or apologetics training (too shallow, for instance).

Finally, some "Christian" schools have academic textbooks and teaching methods that integrate Scripture and a biblical worldview into all subjects. This is finally getting to where it needs to be. But even so, there needs to be another step where the curriculum content actively takes a role to teach and refute the false religions like secular humanism that emanate all around us.

For instance, the classical education curriculum has a framework that is built upon Greek beliefs. Even Christian classical curriculum has a strong emphasis in this area and does not take a stand on a strong biblical creation account — there are exceptions, of course, depending on the headmaster.

If a school says it's Christian, what does that mean? I've seen so many Christian schools that act more like public schools with a Bible class added. They also use secular or compromised textbooks and will accept any student into their school. In some cases, these schools are more focused on high academic ACT/SAT scores.

See why it's important to do your homework? You should be looking for curricula or school programs that are based on a biblical worldview and challenge the students to think critically in all areas.

Final Thoughts

Schooling is a hard decision because there are so many factors to consider! One day we all will stand before God and give an account of our days on this earth, including how we brought up our children. Make sure you will be able to say without a doubt that you did your very best to raise your child as the Lord commanded.

Even if parents send their children to school (even a great biblically based school), it is never to be the school's place to be the primary training center for these children. I see far too many parents basically letting the schools raise their children. We live in such a busy culture, but your children should never be overlooked or sidelined just because you think they're receiving their training in school. Maybe it's time to re-look at your priorities.

The school is to never take the place of home teaching and training — it should be a partnership. Children need the instruction and example by parents in the home as a foundation on which the school and church may build upon.

When your home life, school life, and church match up at a foundational level, you have created a very powerful environment in which to raise your child biblically. The family, church, and school should all have the same goal:

> Until we all attain to the unity of the faith and of the knowledge of the Son of God, to mature manhood, to the measure of the stature of the fullness of Christ, so that we may no longer be children, tossed to and fro by the waves and carried about by every wind of doctrine, by human cunning, by craftiness in deceitful schemes. Rather, speaking the truth in love, we are to grow up in every way into him who is the head, into Christ (Ephesians 4:13–15).

BACK TO
THE TWELVE STONES

> *"Take twelve stones from here out of the midst of
> the Jordan, from the very place where the priests'
> feet stood firmly, and bring them over with you
> and lay them down in the place where you lodge
> tonight" (Joshua 4:3).*

❧

I began this book by discussing how easy it is to not
pass on a godly legacy to the next generation. And
it only takes one generation to lose such a spiritual
legacy. Let's again consider the very sober reminder
concerning Joshua and the twelve stones.

Joshua led the Israelites across the Jordan
River. This was a miracle God performed for the
people so they could cross this normally fast-flowing river. After they crossed the river, God told

Joshua to have twelve men take twelve stones from the river:

> When all the nation had finished passing over the Jordan, the Lord said to Joshua, "Take twelve men from the people, from each tribe a man, and command them, saying, 'Take twelve stones from here out of the midst of the Jordan, from the very place where the priests' feet stood firmly, and bring them over with you and lay them down in the place where you lodge tonight.' " Then Joshua called the twelve men from the people of Israel, whom he had appointed, a man from each tribe. And Joshua said to them, "Pass on before the ark of the Lord your God into the midst of the Jordan, and take up each of you a stone upon his shoulder, according to the number of the tribes of the people of Israel, that this may be a sign among you. When your children ask in time to come, 'What do those stones mean to you?' then you shall tell them that the waters of the Jordan were cut off before the ark of the covenant of the Lord. When it passed over the Jordan, the waters of the Jordan were cut off. So these stones shall be to the people of Israel a memorial forever" (Joshua 4:1–7).

Joshua did as the Lord commanded him. Then we read:

> And those twelve stones, which they took out of the Jordan, Joshua set up at Gilgal. And he said to the people of Israel, "When your children ask their fathers in times to come, 'What do these stones mean?' then you shall let your children know, 'Israel passed over this Jordan on dry ground.' For the LORD your God dried up the waters of the Jordan for you until you passed over, as the LORD your God did to the Red Sea, which he dried up for us until we passed over, so that all the peoples of the earth may know that the hand of the LORD is mighty, that you may fear the LORD your God forever" (Joshua 4:20–24).

These stones were to be a memorial so when their children asked, "What do these stones mean?" they were to be reminded of what God did for the people. Humans are so apt to forget, and God wanted the Israelites to pass on what He did to the coming generations. Not only that, but these stones were also to be a witness to the "peoples of the earth." In other words, the Israelites were to teach the children about this miracle of God and also to tell the world who God is and what He did for them.

When we get to the Book of Judges, we read what I believe is one of the saddest passages in Scripture.

> And all that generation also were gathered to their fathers. And there arose another generation after them who did not know the LORD or the work that he had done for Israel. And the people of Israel did what was evil in the sight of the LORD and served the Baals. And they abandoned the LORD, the God of their fathers, who had brought them out of the land of Egypt. They went after other gods, from among the gods of the peoples who were around them, and bowed down to them. And they provoked the LORD to anger. They abandoned the LORD and served the Baals and the Ashtaroth (Judges 2:10–13).

When Joshua and the generation of adults who experienced the miracle of the crossing of the river Jordan, the next generation abandoned God and served pagan gods. The spiritual legacy was not passed on as it should have been. This is a reminder that it only takes one generation to lose a godly legacy. When one reads through Psalm 78, we read how God reminds the fathers to teach the coming generations. But the Psalm also tells us that the fathers forgot to do this.

My challenge to each of us is this: Are we doing all we can to pass on a godly legacy to the coming generations?

When we opened the Ark Encounter themed attraction, as part of the opening ceremony, the board members of the ministry of Answers in Genesis laid twelve stones on top of each other. I informed the guests that the Ark is our twelve stones. The Ark (and the Creation Museum) are there to remind people of the truth of God's Word and the gospel. These leading Christian attractions were built to help parents train their children in a godly legacy and to impact the world with God's Word and the saving gospel of Jesus Christ.

The twelve stones are now a permanent monument at the Ark Encounter near the queue entrance under the life-size Ark. I love to see families, adults and children, getting their photographs taken in front of these twelve stones so they can discuss the account of Joshua and the twelve stones and what this means to them. Now you've probably figured out why we called our Christian School Twelve

Stones Christian academy. Here is a photograph of some of the Twelve Stones students in front of the monument:

In 2014, an atheist speaking in Australia stated, "Change is always one generation away. So if we can plant the seeds of doubt in our children, religion will go away in a generation, or at least largely go away — and that's what I think we have an obligation to do."

Atheists are out to capture the hearts and minds of your children. And sadly, they are being very successful with the majority of children.

I challenge us all to think how we could be applying "What do those stones mean?" in our own lives/families.

Children at the Grand Canyon ask how the rock layers and canyon were formed — remind them of the Flood of Noah's day and counter the signs teaching millions of years. Children ask why there's death, disease, and suffering in the world — remind them of what sin has done and that the fallen world is our fault, not God's fault. When children ask where babies come from — remind them of God's Word, how He knits us together in our mother's wombs, and that we're "fearfully and wonderfully made." The questions are endless. And we need to continually remind our children of the truth of God's Word.

How is your spiritual legacy measuring up to what God has instructed us to do with the children He has entrusted to us to train for Him?

> Behold, children are a heritage [gift] from the LORD, the fruit of the womb a reward (Psalm 127:3).

INTERVIEW
WITH MALLY HAM

> *Author's Note: I asked Avery Foley, a writer and
> speaker with Answers in Genesis, to interview
> my wife, Mally, on her perspective of the history
> of the AiG ministry and the Ham family.*
>
> *"Neither of us would have envisaged that this
> is what the Lord was going to do, and if we'd
> known, we would have run a million miles."*

∾

On December 30, 1972, a beautiful young woman
named Mally said "I do" to a lanky university student, studiously working to become a teacher like his
father. Mally worked, supporting her new husband
as he finished his degree, before moving with him
to the small country town of Dalby, Australia, for

265

his first teaching appointment. There she imagined her life, settled in rural Australia, surrounded by a brood of children, her husband shaping young minds in the science class of the local high school.

That vision was not to be. God had other ideas for the young couple. While they were dating, Ken was given the little yellow book (pictured on page 53) that first excited him, awakening him to issue of death before sin if the millions of years are true. Soon after, Ken heard about *The Genesis Flood,* and he found a copy in a local Christian bookstore. Ken was so excited, Mally figured she'd go along with her new husband's interest, never imagining where it would lead.

Then, in 1975, at the Baptist church in Dalby, Ken first gave a presentation on creation, evolution, and the age of the earth. This talk was the genesis of what would become the ministry of Answers in Genesis.

In 1976, Ken and Mally both believed God was calling them from Dalby to the coastal city of Brisbane. There Ken continued teaching and gave his first creation seminar in 1977. Mally, home tending their young son, Nathan, missed the seminar. At this program, Ken displayed his collection of creation books and resources on a table at the back.

People were hungry for more answers, so Ken approached Mally in 1977 about needing a bookshop. Mally agreed their home could become part bookshop.

Books soon took over the small house where Ken, Mally, Nathan, and new baby Renee lived. Boxes spilled down the hall and Renee moved to Nathan's room so her bedroom could be used to store the growing collection. Much to Mally's dismay, the collection of books soon attracted some very unwelcome visitors — cockroaches.

It was obvious they needed a new solution. Stepping out in faith, Ken and Mally obtained an additional loan on their house and converted their patio into a bookstore. Mally recalls that, at the time, they thought they had it all. Never could they have imagined that tiny bookstore was just the beginning.

By this time, Ken was traveling on weekends, packing the vehicle full of books Saturday morning, driving many hours, speaking Saturday night and Sunday morning, then driving back Sunday evening, to wake up Monday morning ready to teach his class. Mally recalls the first time Ken left for one of these trips, just weeks after Renee was born. She was terrified to be left alone and asked the wife of Ken's fellow creation speaker to come and stay with her. They had a lovely time, but Mally quickly realized she couldn't have someone come every time Ken left. Searching the Scriptures, Mally found comfort in God's promises, particularly in the Psalms, and chose to trust that God would care for her and her young children.

In 1979, Ken and Mally began discussing the possibility of going full-time in creation ministry. Leaving a secure job of teaching was frightening, but they both realized Ken traveling all weekend was too much for him, and God was calling them to step out in faith. While driving in the car on the way home from visiting friends, Mally read from Matthew 6:

> Therefore I tell you, do not be anxious about your life, what you will eat or what you will drink, nor about your body, what you will put on. Is not life more than food, and the body more than clothing? Look at the birds of the air: they neither sow nor reap nor gather into barns, and yet your heavenly Father feeds them. Are you not of more value than they? And which of you by being anxious can add a single hour to his span of life? And why are you anxious about clothing? Consider the lilies

> of the field, how they grow: they neither toil
> nor spin, yet I tell you, even Solomon in all his
> glory was not arrayed like one of these. But
> if God so clothes the grass of the field, which
> today is alive and tomorrow is thrown into the
> oven, will he not much more clothe you, O
> you of little faith? Therefore do not be anxious,
> saying, "What shall we eat?" or "What shall
> we drink?" or "What shall we wear?" For the
> Gentiles seek after all these things, and your
> heavenly Father knows that you need them
> all. But seek first the kingdom of God and
> his righteousness, and all these things will be
> added to you.

The decision was made. They were going full-time.

Mally says those first years were a blur. Ken was often gone speaking, including trips to America that would last several weeks at a time, the kids were little and kept her busy, and money was tight. Mally shares, "Being home alone was really hard, but you just do it one day at a time and do what you have to do." And God was faithful. He provided for their needs, including using a member of their church who brought baskets of fruit and vegetables by each week. Mally knew, just as Ken knew, that this ministry was what God had called them to and, no matter the challenges and sacrifices, they were in this together.

Then Ken returned from a trip to America and told Mally, "We need to move to America. We need to get the message out in America." At that time, America was the center of the Christian world, and if you wanted to be effective, you had to be there. Mally shares this was her biggest "Red Sea moment." It was a huge step — leaving everything familiar, their family and friends — to travel across the world to the United States.

In just six months, they downsized everything they owned and prepared for the big move. As they packed and prepared, they both wondered, "Is this really what God wants us to do?" (See chapter five for the story of how God confirmed to both of them that this was truly where He was calling their family.)

The family of six (to become a family of seven in 1988) soon settled in San Diego, California. Surrounded by eucalyptus trees, bottle brush trees, and other Aussie plants, Mally was comforted each day with a reminder of her Australian homeland. But seven years (and one more baby) later, God called the Ham family to step out in faith once again —

this time to move to northern Kentucky to start the ministry of Answers in Genesis.

For Mally, this move was even harder in some ways than the move from Australia had been. Kentucky, with its four seasons (including winter!) was very different, and many of the new friends they had made were back in California. But, again, God sustained them. As Mally shared the story of AiG from her perspective, with all the challenges they faced, she continually said, "You do what you have to do, and the Lord looks after you."

Doing what the Lord called them to do wasn't (and still isn't) without sacrifice for Ken, Mally, and the five children. "For us as a family, Kenny being gone all the time and traveling all the time is a big sacrifice. Being away from our family in Australia, especially when we first moved and there were no cellphones and no computers, made it very hard to keep in contact with family. In those early days, it was really hard. It's easier now than what it used to be." But Mally has no regrets — this is what God called both Ken and Mally to, and they joyfully serve Him in the ministry He's entrusted them with.

Answers in Genesis has always been a family ministry. Mally jokes that "I'm the real CEO because I tell him what to do and how to do it." In the early days, Mally recalls the whole family sitting on the floor stuffing envelopes to mail out to supporters or traveling together to support Ken as he spoke. Mally even tried homeschooling on the road, but with little success — the kids were far more interested in what was going on outside the windows! Today, four of the five children and some of the grandchildren work for Answers in Genesis, and the whole family loves the ministry and champions the message.

After nearly 48 years of marriage, Mally looks back on their many years together and all that God has accomplished and thinks, "Wow. I am blown away with what the Lord has done. Kenny and I are still part of the ministry, and our kids are too, but we're just little pieces of the ministry. This ministry is God's ministry and He's been faithful. He's seen us through."

Mally's true loves are obvious after just a few minutes of conversation — she loves her husband (whom she describes as "a big softie who would do anything for me, and anything for the kids. If he could possibly do it, he would do it."), her five children, her eighteen grandchildren, and, above all else, her Lord and His Word.

Raising five children with a husband who was frequently gone had its challenges, and the whole family sacrificed for the AiG ministry to be what it is. But it had its positives as well. The Ham children grew up knowing many great theologians and scientists who loved God and believed His Word. They watched both their mother and father stand solidly on the Word of God, never wavering. They saw (and continue to see) God provide for their needs and bring them through many "Red Sea" events.

Mally believes their stand on God's Word has impacted her children greatly and is a big reason why all five love and serve the Lord today. Mothers, she says, should realize that the "most important thing for a mom to focus on is allowing God's Word to saturate every part of your kids' thinking. That has to be first and foremost."

Ken says another reason their children are who they are today is because of who Mally is — "She's always been there for the kids, she's totally selfless, always putting the needs of others before her own, she's generous and would do anything to help anyone. Her constant devotion, stand on the Word, and counsel from Scripture have helped shape five hearts to love the Lord Jesus and continue passing the knowledge of the Lord along to the next generation."

While having your husband recognized every time you go anywhere isn't exactly normal, Mally says she doesn't feel like she's married to a famous Christian speaker. "The Lord has gifted him in a mighty way. I do not feel like the wife of a famous speaker who heads up this ministry. We're just down-to-earth people from Sunnybank, Australia. That's who we see ourselves as and that's who we are."

Mally has heard her husband speak countless times and she loves it (especially his "Creation vs. Evolution: Why it Matters" and "One Race, One Blood" talks and his "Dinosaurs for Kids" program with Buddy Davis). Afterward, Mally often stands quietly off to the side and listens to the testimonies of countless individuals and families as they shake Ken's hand. Her favorite stories are from parents who say, "I heard your dinosaur talk when I was just a little kid, and it impacted me and now I'm raising my children on your materials." It reminds her, "This is why we did it. This is why we sacrificed so much."

But to hear the story of Answers in Genesis, the Creation Museum, and the Ark Encounter isn't really to hear the story of the Ham family. It's to hear the story of what God has done through humble servants who love Him and are willing to do what it takes to obey His call on their lives. After nearly five decades of marriage to a man some would call "controversial" for his stand on God's Word, serving alongside him in a worldwide ministry that built a one-of-its-kind Creation Museum and a life-size Noah's Ark, Mally says, "We have had an awesome ride together. It's a crazy ride with being a part of this ministry and neither of us would have envisaged that this is what the Lord was going to do, and if we'd known, we would have run a million miles. We honestly couldn't have done this on our own strength, without the Lord going ahead and opening doors and orchestrating things and giving us little glimpses."

THE REVELATION OF A LEGACY

> *"Dad understood the foundational importance of the inerrant, infallible, inspired Word of God."*

Sometimes, a single phone call can change your whole life . . . and change it forever. In June of 1995, we all knew "the call" was coming and prepared ourselves as best we could. In many ways we had had a lifetime to prepare for it as we observed Mum and Dad walk with God in light of eternity, but this felt different, for now Dad was preparing to take the final step. He had been sick off and on for some time, and this time we knew that he would not be getting better.

Still, as ready as we were, and as ready as Dad was, the phone calls seemed to stop the rotation of earth, dislodging everything that seemed immovable. Dad entered eternity and embraced the One whom he had believed, loved, and served by faith.

My mum and siblings in Australia escorted Dad to the threshold of eternal life; I was sitting in a hotel room in Indianapolis, Indiana. The call came on the 9th of June. It was my brother Robert. The news grabbed my heart, and I sank onto the bed, doing my best just to breathe. So many things were flashing through my mind, but it was like being in a daze. Nothing connected. In my room and outside my window, everything appeared to be the same, but with that one brief phone call, everything was different.

The phone rang once more — it was the local Christian radio station calling for an interview to promote the seminar I was speaking at. I answered the questions and tried to act as my normal self, but nothing felt normal. As if on autopilot, I picked up my briefcase and walked across the road and parking lot to the Indianapolis Convention Center. It seemed like such a long walk, almost as if time had stopped completely. I took a deep breath, entered the auditorium, took my place at the podium in front of hundreds of people, and somehow began my lecture. . . .

Dad and I had talked many times over the years as to what I should do if he were to die while I was conducting a seminar. Knowing my father was seriously ill, I could have cancelled the seminar and traveled home (36 hours usually, including around 20 hours of flying). Dad had told me on more than one occasion that he had trained us to love God's Word and there was nothing more important than to tell people about Christ. He said, "Kenneth, if I die, there's really no point in coming back because I won't be here. It will be more important to preach God's Word so others can join me in heaven."

So, I had decided to stay and speak at the seminar — this is what my father would want, and I wanted to honor his request. By the grace of God, I was able to complete my messages that day and over the next several days.

Meanwhile, a burial service for family and close friends was conducted at the cemetery a few miles from our family home. A close friend videotaped the service so I could view it later. When the seminars were complete, Mally and I boarded a plane with our children and flew to Australia for a special memorial service for Dad on the 25th of June. It was an emotional homecoming as I embraced Mum and faced my father's physical absence for the first time. I had come home to give honor to my dad, but it turned out that he had one last earthly gift for me.

In the months before Dad died, he had constructed a model of Noah's Ark. True to the dimensions in Scripture, he had built the small craft to scale and weighted it properly so that it could withstand waves without turning over. My father wasn't a carpenter, but he put his heart and soul into making this model something special. When I arrived home, it was there, floating in the pool, flying miniature flags from both Australia and the United States.

The ark my father built is now in a Legacy Exhibit in the Creation Museum. This small exhibit features my father's Bible showing some of his notes in Genesis, the ark he built me, a photo of Mum and Dad, and an old video clip of my father. Each time I look at this exhibit, I am reminded of the inheritance my parents gave me — an inheritance that is far more valuable than silver or gold. They left an everlasting spiritual inheritance: a love for the Creator and Savior and His infallible Word. I've seen people standing in front of this exhibit, and I've asked them, "What does this mean to you?" I've had a number say, "It challenges me about what legacy I'm leaving in this world."

At the memorial service, my five brothers and sisters and I shared our testimonies concerning Dad. We all used different terminology and phraseology — but our words conveyed the same basic theme:

> Dad never knowingly wanted to compromise the Word of God.

> Dad always stood up for what he believed.

> Dad taught his children to love the Word of God.

> Dad always wanted God's Word to be in authority over the fallible words of man.

> Dad hated compromise and would actively contend for the Christian faith.

> Dad understood the foundational importance of the inerrant, infallible, inspired Word of God.

This was what we shared about our Dad. At the end of the service, a dear friend of the family came up to me and said, "After a service like that, I'm challenged to go home and ask my children what they're going to say about me when I'm dead!" His question sparked my vision for this book, knowing that the question is one that all who desire to raise godly children in this ungodly world should ask. What will your children say about you when you die?

From the beginning of his legacy on Thursday Island in 1928 to the revelation of his legacy at this memorial service in 1995, God used this simple and devoted man to reach a family . . . and then reach the world for the truth and for the Creator. May any and all glory and honor go to the Lord my father served. May any and all thanks go not to my father, but to his Father . . . for that is the way that both of them would want it.

> Praise the LORD!
> Praise the LORD from the heavens;
>   praise him in the heights!
> Praise him, all his angels;
>   praise him, all his hosts!
> Praise him, sun and moon,
>   praise him, all you shining stars!
> Praise him, you highest heavens,
>   and you waters above the heavens!
> Let them praise the name of the LORD!
>   For he commanded and they were created.
> And he established them forever and ever;

he gave a decree, and it shall not pass away.
Praise the LORD from the earth,
    you great sea creatures and all deeps,
fire and hail, snow and mist,
    stormy wind fulfilling his word!
Mountains and all hills,
    fruit trees and all cedars!
Beasts and all livestock,
    creeping things and flying birds!
Kings of the earth and all peoples,
    princes and all rulers of the earth!
Young men and maidens together,
    old men and children!
Let them praise the name of the LORD,
    for his name alone is exalted;
    his majesty is above earth and heaven.
        (Psalm 148:1–13)

On the fifteenth of November 2019, our dear mother left this earth to be in the presence of her Savior. At her memorial service, the siblings (except for my brother Robert, who went to be with the Lord seven years after Dad died) really expressed the same things we did about our Dad. This is what I wrote about Mum on our Answers in Genesis website:

Eternally Grateful: A Tribute to Norma Ham

by Ken Ham on November 15, 2019

Today, Friday, November 15 (EST), in Queensland, Australia, my mother went through the shadow of death to be with her Savior for eternity! Norma Ham was almost ninety-two.

Thank you all for your prayers. We are so thankful we could be here with all my siblings (except for our brother Robert, who went to be with the Lord seventeen years ago).

As I think about my precious mother right now with a heavy heart, I recall the time she shared her views of life, death, and eternity with me. In fact, we videotaped Mum in her Australian home on November 25, 2014, as she talked about her life. I trust the short video clip attached from that time will minister to you.

She is one of the true saints! I think of the Apostle Paul's words, "Greet every saint in Christ Jesus" (Philippians 4:21). Mum devoted herself to my late dad, their six children, twenty grandchildren, and forty-eight great-grandchildren. She prayed for her whole family every day by name. I have vivid memories of my mother teaching me to pray as a young child. She also loved teaching me the words of the hymn composed in 1839 and published in 1841, "Jesus, Tender Shepherd, Hear Me." I've never forgotten those words:

Jesus, tender Shepherd, hear me;
Bless Thy little lamb tonight:
Through the darkness be Thou near me,
Keep me safe till morning light.
All this day Thy hand has led me,
And I thank Thee for Thy care;
Thou hast warmed me, clothed and fed me;
Listen to my evening prayer.
Let my sins be all forgiven;
Bless the friends I love so well:
Take us all at last to heaven,
Happy there with Thee to dwell.[1]

---

1. Mary Duncan, née Lundie composed this hymn for her children in 1839, and was first published in her *Memoir*, 1841 (edition 1843, p. 311).

There are many things she taught me that I'll always remember, such as the following principles:

- It's only what is done for Jesus that lasts.
- Put God first, others second, and yourself last.

I can truly say that the ministry of AiG, the Creation Museum, and the Ark Encounter, which each year impact tens of millions of people around the world, are a legacy of my Mum and Dad. They taught their children to stand boldly and unashamedly on the Word of God. They would never knowingly compromise God's Word — they hated such compromise. My parents taught me to "smell" liberal theology a million miles away!

My parents started Sunday schools and organized many evangelistic programs in Australia that reached children and adults with the saving gospel. Only God knows the impact their faithfulness to His Word and the gospel has had on a multitude of people.

I will miss you, Mum — but I look forward to seeing you in heaven!

It's been hard being across the ocean for so many years. But I praise the Lord for the technology we have today like Facetime so that I could often stay in touch with Mum. When we heard that she was failing, my wife, Mally, and I used Facetime to tell her we loved her. She was conscious but couldn't speak, yet she managed to mouth the words back: "I love you." We then flew to Australia to be at her side.

Until we meet again, Mum . . . in glory!

ADDITIONAL READING ON A BIBLICAL WORDVIEW

What Is a Biblical Worldview?

by Ken Ham and Stacia McKeever

The history as recorded in the Bible has been attacked by our increasingly secular culture. As a result, recent generations have been brought up to see the Bible as a book that contains many interesting stories and religious teaching but has no connection to reality.

This limited viewpoint helps explain why there are so many questions about how the Bible can explain dinosaurs, fossils, death, suffering, and many other topics that relate to our real world.

This chapter will outline the major events of the past (and even the future) — the "7 C's of History"

— that are foundational to the Bible's important message and demonstrate how the Bible connects to the real world.

Creation

God created the heavens, the earth, and all that is in them in six normal-length days around 6,000 years ago. His completed creation was "very good" (Genesis 1:31), and all the original animals (including dinosaurs) and the first two humans (Adam and Eve) ate only plants (Genesis 1:29–30). Life was perfect and not yet affected by the curse — death, violence, disease, sickness, thorns, and fear had no part in the original creation.

After he was finished creating, God "rested" (or stopped) from his work, although He continues to uphold the creation (Colossians 1:17). His creation of all things in six days and resting on the seventh set a pattern for our week, which He designed for us to follow.

> *GOD CREATED THE HEAVENS, THE EARTH, AND ALL THAT IS IN THEM IN SIX NORMAL-LENGTH DAYS AROUND 6,000 YEARS AGO.*

The science of "information theory" confirms

that first statement of the Bible, "In the beginning God created. . . ." DNA is the molecule of heredity, part of a staggeringly complex system, more information-dense than that in the most efficient supercomputer. Since the information in our DNA can only come from a source of greater information (or intelligence), there must have been something other than matter in the beginning. This other source must have no limit to its intelligence; in fact, it must be an ultimate source of intelligence from which all things have come. The Bible tells us there is such a source — God. Since God has no beginning and no end and knows all (Psalm 147:5), it makes sense that God is the source of the information we see all around us! This fits with real science, just as we would expect.[1]

In Genesis, God created things "after their kinds." And this is what we observe today: great variation within different "kinds" (e.g., dogs, cats, elephants, etc.), but not one kind changing into another, as molecules-to-man evolution requires.[2]

---

1. For a more in-depth analysis of the complexity of DNA and information theory, see www.AnswersInGenesis.org/go/information_theory.

2. For more information, see www.AnswersInGenesis.org/go/kinds.

Corruption

After God completed His perfect creation, He told Adam that he could eat from any tree in the Garden of Eden (Genesis 2:8) except one — the Tree of the Knowledge of Good and Evil. He warned Adam that death would be the punishment for disobedience (Genesis 2:17). Instead of listening to the command of his Creator, Adam chose to rebel, eating the fruit from the tree (Genesis 3:6). Because our Holy God must punish sin, He sacrificed animal(s) to make coverings for Adam and Eve, and He sent the first couple from the garden, mercifully denying them access to the Tree of Life so that they would not live forever in their sinful state.

Adam's sin ushered death, sickness, and sorrow into the once-perfect creation (Genesis 3:19; Romans 5:12). God also pronounced a curse on the world (Genesis 3; Romans 8:20–22). As a result, the world that we now live in is a decaying remnant — a corruption — of the beautiful, righteous world that Adam and Eve originally called home. We see the results of this corruption all around us in the form of carnivorous animals, mutations, sickness, disease, and death.[3] The good news is that, rather than

---

3. For more information, see www.AnswersInGenesis.org/go/curse.

leave His precious handiwork without hope, God graciously promised to one day send a Redeemer who would buy back His people from the curse of sin (Genesis 3:15).

Catastrophe

As the descendants of Adam and Eve married and filled the earth with offspring, their wickedness was great (Genesis 6:5). God judged their sin by sending a global Flood to destroy all men, animals, creatures that moved along the ground, and birds of the air (Genesis 6:7). Those God chose to enter the Ark — Noah, his family, and land-dwelling representatives of the animal kingdom (including dinosaurs) — were saved from the watery catastrophe.

There was plenty of room in the huge vessel for tens of thousands of animals — even dinosaurs (the average dinosaur was only the size of a bison, and Noah didn't have to take fully grown adults of the large dinosaurs). Noah actually needed only about 7,000 animals on the Ark to represent all the distinct kinds of land-dwelling animals.[4]

This earth-covering event has left its mark even today. From the thousands of feet of sedimentary

---

4. For more information see https://answersingenesis.org/noahs-ark/how-could-all-animals-fit-ark/.

rock found around the world to the billions of dead things buried in rock layers (fossils), the Flood reminds us even today that our righteous God cannot — and will not — tolerate sin, while the Ark reminds us that He provides a way of salvation from sin's punishment. The rainbows we experience today remind us of God's promise never again to destroy the earth with water (Genesis 9:13–15). Incidentally, if the Flood were a local event (rather than global in extent), as some claim, then God has repeatedly broken His promise since we continue to experience local flooding even today.[5]

Confusion

After the Flood, God commanded Noah and his family — the only humans left in the world — and the animals to fill the earth (Genesis 8:17). However, the human race once again disobeyed God's command and built a tower, which they hoped would keep them together (Genesis 11:3–4). So, around 100 years after the Flood waters had retreated, God brought a confusion (a multiplicity) of languages in place of the common language the people shared, causing them to spread out over the earth. The different languages created suddenly at

5.   For more information, see www.AnswersInGenesis.org/go/flood.

Babel (Genesis 10–11) could each subsequently give rise to many more. Languages gradually change, so when a group of people break up into several groups that no longer interact, after a few centuries they may each speak a different (but related) language. Today, we have thousands of languages but only 95–100 language "families."[6]

> ALL THE TRIBES AND NATIONS IN THE WORLD TODAY HAVE DESCENDED FROM THESE VARIOUS GROUPS.

All the tribes and nations in the world today have descended from these various groups. Despite what you may have been led to believe about our superficial differences, we really are all "one blood" (Acts 17:26) — descendants of Adam and Eve through Noah and his family — and all, therefore, are in need of salvation from sin.

God had created Adam and Eve with the ability to produce children with a variety of different characteristics. This ability was passed on through Noah and his family. As the people scattered, they took with them genetic variations for certain

---

6. For more information, see www.AnswersInGenesis.org/go/linguistics.

characteristics — e.g., height, the amount of pigment for hair and skin shade (by the way, we all have the same pigment, just more or less of it), and so on.

In fact, the Human Genome Project supports this biblical teaching that there is only one biological race of humans. As one report says, "It is clear that what is called 'race' . . . reflects just a few continuous traits determined by a tiny fraction of our genes."[7] The basic principles of genetics explain various shades of one skin color (not different colors) and how the distinct people groups (e.g., American Indians, Australian Aborigines) came about because of the event at the Tower of Babel. The creation and Flood legends of these peoples from all around the world also confirm the Bible's anthropology to be true.

Christ

God's perfect creation was corrupted by Adam when he disobeyed God, ushering sin and death into the world. Because of Adam's disobedience and because we have all sinned personally, we are all deserving of the death penalty and need a Savior (Romans 5:12).

---

7. S. Pääbo, "The Human Genome and Our View of Ourselves," *Science* 29, no. 5507 (2001): 1219–1220.

As mentioned before, God did not leave His precious — but corrupted — creation without hope. He promised to one day send Someone who would take away the penalty for sin, which is death (Genesis 3:15; Ezekiel 18:4; Romans 6:23).

God killed at least one animal in the garden of Eden because of the sin of Adam; subsequently, Adam's descendants sacrificed animals. Such sacrifices could only cover sin — they pointed toward the time when the One whom God would send (Hebrews 9) would make the ultimate sacrifice.

When God gave Moses the Law, people began to see that they could never measure up to God's standard of perfection (Romans 3:20) — if they broke any part of the Law, the result was the same as breaking all of it (James 2:10). They needed Someone to take away their imperfection and present them faultless before God's throne (Romans 5:9; 1 Peter 3:18).

In line with God's purpose and plan for everything, He sent His promised Savior at just the right time (Galatians 4:4). There was a problem, however. All humans are descended from Adam, and therefore, all humans are born with sin. God's chosen One had to be perfect, as well as infinite, to take away the infinite penalty for sin.

God solved this "problem" by sending His Son, Jesus Christ — completely human and completely God. Think of it: the Creator of the universe (John 1:1–3, 14) became part of His creation so that He might save His people from their sins!

Jesus fulfilled more than 50 prophecies made about Him centuries before, showing He was the One promised over 4,000 years before by His Father (Genesis 3:15). While He spent over 30 years on earth, He never once sinned — He did nothing wrong. He healed many people, fed huge crowds, and taught thousands of listeners about their Creator God and how to be reconciled to Him. He even confirmed the truth of Genesis by explaining that marriage is between one man and one woman (Matthew 19:3–6, quoting Genesis 1:27 and 2:24).

Cross

Jesus is called the "Last Adam" in 1 Corinthians 15:45. While Adam disobeyed God's command not to eat the forbidden fruit, Jesus fulfilled the Creator's purpose that He die for sinners.

The first Adam brought death into the world through his disobedience; the Last Adam brought eternal life with God through His obedience (1 Corinthians 15:21–22).

Because God is perfectly holy, He must punish sin — either the sinner himself or a substitute to bear His wrath. Jesus bore God's wrath for our sin by dying in our place on the Cross (Isaiah 53:6). The Lamb of God (John 1:29; Revelation 5:12) was sacrificed once for all (Hebrews 7:27), so that all those who believe in Him will be saved from the ultimate penalty for sin (eternal separation from God) and will live with Him forever.

Jesus Christ, the Creator of all things (John 1:1–3; Colossians 1:15–16), was not defeated by death. He rose three days after He was crucified, showing that He has power over all things, including death, the "last enemy" (1 Corinthians 15:26). As Paul wrote, "O death, where is your victory? O death, where is your sting? . . . But thanks be to God, who gives us the victory through our Lord Jesus Christ" (1 Corinthians 15:55–57).

WHEN WE BELIEVE IN CHRIST AND UNDERSTAND WHAT HE HAS DONE FOR US, WE ARE PASSED FROM DEATH INTO LIFE.

When we believe in Christ and understand what He has done for us, we are passed from death into life (John 5:24). The names of those who receive Him are written in the Lamb's Book of Life (Revelation 13:8; 17:8) — when they die, they will go to be with Him forever (John 3:16).

Just as "science" cannot prove that Jesus rose from the dead, it also cannot prove that God created everything in six days. In fact, "science" can't prove any event from history because it is limited in dealings about the past. Historical events are known to be true because of reliable eyewitness accounts. In fact, there are reliable eyewitness accounts that Jesus' tomb was empty after three days and that He later appeared to as many as 500 people at once (1 Corinthians 15:6). Of course, we know that both the Resurrection and creation in six days are true because God, who cannot lie, states in His Word that these things happened.

While the secular history of millions of years isn't true, and evolutionary geology, biology, anthropology, astronomy, etc., do not stand the test of observational science, the Bible's history, from Genesis 1 onward, is true. The Bible's geology, biology, anthropology, astronomy, etc., are confirmed by observational science. Therefore, the fact that the Bible's history is true should challenge people to seriously consider the Bible's message of salvation that is based in this history.

Consummation

Death has been around almost as long as humans have. Romans 8 tells us that the whole of creation is suffering because of Adam's sin. As terrible as things are, however, they are not a permanent part of creation.

God, in His great mercy, has promised not to leave His creation in its sinful state. He has promised to do away with the corruption that Adam brought into the world. He has promised to remove, in the future, the curse He placed on His creation (Revelation 22:3) and to make a new heaven and a new earth (2 Peter 3:13). In this new place there will be no death, crying, or pain (Revelation 21:4).

Those who have repented and believed in what Jesus did for them on the Cross can look forward to the consummation of God's kingdom — this new heaven and earth — knowing they will enjoy God forever in a wonderful place. In the future, God will take away the corruption that was introduced in the garden of Eden, giving us once again a perfect place to live!

A worldview based on a proper understanding of the history of the world, as revealed in the Bible, is what every Christian needs to combat our society's evolutionary propaganda.

DISCIPLINING CHILDREN GOD'S WAY

by David Chakranarayan and Ken Ham

ဢ

Parents, if you desire to demonstrate biblical love to your children, then exercise biblical discipline. Our culture would benefit greatly from parents disciplining their children God's way.

Many Christians have known for a long time that discipline of children is a problem in our American culture — and now some Australian education experts are beginning to agree! An article from an Australian news source is titled "Education experts claim discipline system in state schools is 'new-age and politically correct.' "[1] In it, education experts argued that the disciplinary measures in Australian schools are not working.

---

1. Sarah Vogler and Rob Kidd, "Education Experts Claim Discipline System in State Schools is 'New-Age and Politically Correct,'" http://www.couriermail.com.au/news/queensland/schools-need-discipline-back/story-e6freoof-1226615287525.

Kevin Donnelly, director of the Education Standards Institute, not only identified a problem with the school system, but also suggested that parents "needed to play a bigger role in teaching their children respect for authority."

Surprisingly, he's right! Parents in American culture, like in Australia, do not discipline children God's way. They are not teaching their children respect for authority, and that has left us with many problems. Just as the culture has abandoned the foundation of God's Word for its worldview regarding such issues as marriage and the sanctity of life, so also it has abandoned the authority of Scripture in discipline of children.

Secular psychology rejects that children are sinners and instead teaches that children are basically "good." This is a false premise, and it will never lead to the exercise of biblical discipline of children. Children are no different than adults when it comes to sin, "for all have sinned and fall short of the glory of God" (Romans 3:23)

Many people, including some Christians, fail to realize that one God-given aspect of biblical discipline is corporal punishment — and God tells parents to use it in disciplining their children. Of course, there are some people who have abused children with force, and we at Answers in Genesis reject this misuse of corporal punishment.

Biblical Parenting Involves Discipline

Physical punishment performed in a biblical manner is a socially unpopular component of biblical parenting, but there is more to parenting than just corporal punishment. Other aspects to biblical discipline include rewards and disincentives, "do's and don'ts," leadership by example (especially in faithfully following God's Word), and so on.

Throughout the Book of Proverbs, biblical discipline is emphasized as the way to life and wisdom. Below are a variety of proverbs (NKJV) that speak to the issue of disciplining our children:

> For the commandment is a lamp, and the law a light; reproofs of instruction are the way of life (Proverbs 6:23).
>
> Whoever loves instruction loves knowledge, but he who hates correction is stupid (Proverbs 12:1).
>
> He who spares his rod hates his son, but he who loves him disciplines him promptly (Proverbs 13:24).

> Chasten your son while there is hope, and do not set your heart on his destruction (Proverbs 19:18).

> Train up a child in the way he should go, and when he is old he will not depart from it (Proverbs 22:6).

> Foolishness is bound up in the heart of a child; the rod of correction will drive it far from him (Proverbs 22:15).

> Do not withhold correction from a child, for if you beat him with a rod, he will not die. You shall beat him with a rod, and deliver his soul from hell (Proverbs 23:13–14).

> The rod and rebuke give wisdom, but a child left to himself brings shame to his mother (Proverbs 29:15).

> Correct your son, and he will give you rest; yes, he will give delight to your soul (Proverbs 29:17).

As part of the command to exercise biblical discipline, God also instructs parents not to "provoke" their children. In other words, discipline in all its aspects — positive and negative, physical and verbal — should be applied, not abusively, but in a way that encourages the child to become the kind of person God intends (which incidentally is the sort of child both parents and teachers want to see):

> And you, fathers, do not provoke your children to wrath, but bring them up in the training and admonition of the Lord (Ephesians 6:4; NKJV).

> Fathers, do not provoke your children, lest they become discouraged (Colossians 3:21; NKJV).

Love Is the Motivation for Disciplining Children

Any discipline, whether corporal or otherwise, must be motivated by love, being concerned for the best interests of the child. When we discipline our children, we are attempting to teach them wisdom and to show them right from wrong. If we discipline biblically and in love, our children will grow to respect us as parents for it, recognizing that we, too, are under God's authority. Furthermore, they will learn to respect those in authority outside of the home, whether teachers, government officials, or employers.

The Bible commands us to discipline our children because it is a reflection of how God disciplines believers, who are His children:

> And you have forgotten the exhortation which speaks to you as to sons: "My son, do not despise the chastening of the LORD, nor be discouraged when you are rebuked by Him; for whom the LORD loves He chastens, and scourges every son whom He receives." If you endure chastening, God deals with you as with sons; for what son is there whom a father does not chasten? But if you are without chastening, of which all have become partakers, then you are illegitimate and not sons. Furthermore, we have had human fathers who corrected us, and we paid them respect. Shall we not much more readily be in subjection to the Father of spirits and live? For they indeed for a few days chastened us as seemed best to them, but He for our profit, that we may be partakers of His holiness. Now no chastening seems to be joyful for the present, but painful; nevertheless, afterward it yields the peaceable fruit of righteousness to those who have been trained by it (Hebrews 12:5–11; NKJV).

Hebrews is clear: discipline from God our Father may be unpleasant, but the reward is the "fruit of righteousness." Likewise, when we practice biblical discipline with our children, we demonstrate that we love our children, and it teaches them wisdom and drives away foolishness.

Discipline Does Not Guarantee Godliness

There are, however, many instances when God-honoring parents train their children in God's Word and discipline their children in a godly manner, only to have them rebel later in life. It can be deeply discouraging for parents to see their adult children walking away from the Lord. Parents often feel guilty because they believe such a rebellion was caused by something they failed to do during their children's younger years. However, when we look at Scripture, there are several instances of children rebelling against their parents. The following two accounts exemplify this.

The first account features Hophni and Phineas, the sons of Eli. Eli was a priest in Shiloh who was a personal caregiver to the child Samuel (1 Samuel 1:3). Eli was responsible for the spiritual and religious training of Samuel, who in turn was instrumental in calling Israel to repentance and delivering them from foreign domination. There is no doubt that Eli was a godly man who was seeking to please the Lord. However, his sons did not display the same godly character. Hophni and Phineas served as priests in Shiloh like their father, but they disregarded the duties of priesthood and engaged in illicit behavior (1 Samuel 2). God was not pleased with their actions, and they were eventually slain by the Philistines (1 Samuel 4).

The second account to consider is the parable of the prodigal son (Luke 15:11–31). While this may simply be a fictional narrative, Jesus used it to demonstrate God's love toward sinners. In this parable, the son requests and receives his inheritance from his father and wastes it in sinful living. The prodigal son realizes that the servants in his father's home are living in better conditions than he is. He comes home and is reconciled to his father.

Like these sons of old, our children might make decisions that contradict their godly upbringing. Ultimately, our children will have to make their own personal decision to trust in Christ. Through our discipline, we must teach our children God's grace and obedience that comes with a transformed heart through the power of the gospel.

Exemplifying Christ to Our Children

As parents, we constantly have to evaluate our own sinful behavior in light of who Christ is, evaluating our sinfulness and failures with those of our children and finding victory only in the finished work of Christ on the Cross and His Resurrection from the dead. Our motivation for the discipline of our children is to show them their sinfulness and point them to Christ.

For example, Solomon was the wisest king to ever live — he built a temple for the Lord, ruled during Israel's golden age, and wrote three books in the Old Testament. As one reads the Book of Proverbs, it is very clear that Solomon took his role of king and father very seriously. However, there is a great contrast between what Solomon wrote and how he behaved, and this may have directly contributed to his children's rebellion.

OUR MOTIVATION FOR THE DISCIPLINE OF OUR CHILDREN IS TO SHOW THEM THEIR SINFULNESS AND POINT THEM TO CHRIST.

In an article in *Answers* magazine, the author states, "Solomon accumulated wealth for his own purposes (1 Kings

10:14–23); he imported a great army of the best horses (1 Kings 10:26–29); and he built a great harem of women and became idolatrous (1 Kings 11:1–6)."[2] Similarly, if we as parents are not seeking to be more like Christ, we will continue to fail in leading and disciplining our children. Our shepherding methods must reflect that of the Savior as we protect and provide for our own sheep — our children (John 10).

Parents, if you desire to demonstrate biblical love to your children, then exercise biblical discipline. Our culture as a whole would benefit greatly from parents disciplining their children God's way.

---

2. Steve Ham, "The True Power of Proverbs," *Answers* Vol 8, no.1 https://answersingenesis.org/bible-characters/the-true-power-of-proverbs/.